Helping Every Child in the Early Years

Helping Every Child to Thrive in the Early Years shows how a personalised and relationship-based approach to education and care can help overcome the 'disadvantage gap' in the early years. It examines the challenges that children from disadvantaged backgrounds face and looks at what settings and practitioners can do to enable every child to succeed.

Drawing on the latest research and using the insight gained from many years of working in early education the book considers the impact that disadvantage can have on children's development and argues that building strong relationships with children and families is key to closing the gap.

Chapters cover:

- The different kinds and effects of disadvantage
- The importance of having a clear vision and shared values
- The culture of early years and how it has shaped practice
- Developing strong parent partnerships
- Supporting children with additional needs
- Smooth transitions

Full of practical advice and supporting anecdotes and case studies, this is essential reading for early years practitioners, setting managers and teachers working with children in Reception and KS1.

Maureen Hunt taught for 22 years in Nursery and Infant Schools across Southampton. She went on to work for Action for Children (now NCH) and then as a Regional Lead for Cornwall LA Children's Services. In 2013 Maureen was appointed as Head of Early Years at Achievement for All and developed an award-winning national programme to support Early Years settings to improve outcomes for the most vulnerable and disadvantaged children.

Maureen is currently working as an Independent Education Consultant specialising in Early Years and Primary Education.

Helping Every Child to Thrive in the Early Years

How to Overcome the Effect of Disadvantage

Maureen Hunt

Routledge
Taylor & Francis Group

LONDON AND NEW YORK

Cover image: Cavan Images © Getty Images

First published 2022
by Routledge
4 Park Square, Milton Park, Abingdon, Oxon, OX14 4RN

and by Routledge
605 Third Avenue, New York, NY 10158

Routledge is an imprint of the Taylor & Francis Group, an informa business

© 2022 Maureen Hunt

British Library Cataloguing-in-Publication Data
A catalogue record for this book is available from the British Library

Library of Congress Cataloging-in-Publication Data
A catalog record has been requested for this book

ISBN: 978-0-367-86019-6 (hbk)
ISBN: 978-0-367-86020-2 (pbk)
ISBN: 978-1-003-01646-5 (ebk)

DOI: 10.4324/9781003016465

Typeset in Bembo
by codeMantra

Contents

Lists of figures   *vi*

  Introduction   1

1 What Is Disadvantage?   5

2 The Culture of Early Years   19

3 Inclusion   27

4 Vision and Values   33

5 Parent Partnerships   43

6 Children with Additional Needs   57

7 Ready to Read?   73

8 Transitions   83

  Conclusion   93

Index   95

Figures

1.1   Maslow's hierarchy of needs   9
4.1   Core values   41
5.1   Effects of school compared to effects of parents   46

Introduction

Free the child's potential, and you will transform him into the world.

— *Maria Montessori*

I'll never forget my first teaching appointment and my first Reception class; I was beyond excited. It was my first real full-time job and I put my heart and soul into it, even though I didn't really know what I was doing. I had only been on three teaching practices and inside a school for a total of 12 weeks prior to starting. My first placement was in a school where I was allowed only to observe and help out occasionally and the teaching was always whole class and very formal. My second placement was better, but this one was all group work with no direct teaching to the whole class. Only on my third placement was I allowed to teach and did a mixture of whole class and group work. I probably taught for a total of about three weeks all together before I was given my own class.

To say the reality of being responsible for my own class was a shock is an understatement, as there really was no support or guidance whatsoever. The rest of the school staff seemed unwilling or unconfident to enter the Reception class and I had no teaching assistant, so I was left to my own devices. This was long before the Early Years Foundation Stage (EYFS) and the National Curriculum, the terms differentiation and child-led practice were unheard of and I just muddled through.

There was so much that I hadn't been prepared for or even considered; how to communicate with parents, how to manage different abilities, how to plan day in and day out, what to do about 'naughty children' – it was a steep learning curve. I told myself that after one year I would have it cracked; little did I know then that 40 years later I would still be learning, trying new things and honing

DOI: 10.4324/9781003016465-1

my craft. My 40 years working with children, families and wider professionals have thrown up many challenges especially when working with families that were disadvantaged through poverty and children who had identified special educational needs or disabilities (SEND). To me the education dice seemed to be loaded against these children and I recognised quite early on that they would need a different approach if they were to succeed and flourish. Thus began my passion for working to overcome disadvantage and the ongoing struggle to try and meet their needs given the limited resources, and on occasion direction and guidance from leadership teams that was in direct conflict with my own values of what I believed to be in the child's best interests.

Lots of times I made mistakes, got things wrong and became disheartened; but looking back now I can see that my mistakes were an important part of the journey – they made me address issues, led me to research and make changes in my practice in a way that perhaps wouldn't have happened otherwise. In short, they were often turning points and for that I am grateful.

There is little doubt that in 2021 we have a crisis in education, not just because we are in the middle of a global pandemic and so many children have missed out on their education, but also, despite all the emphasis on standards made by successive governments and the fact that overall pupil attainment is rising, there is no progress in closing the disadvantage gap. The pandemic has shone yet another spotlight on the impact disadvantage has on education

> many of the world's children – particularly those in poorer households – do not have internet access, personal computers, TVs or even radio at home, amplifying the effects of existing learning inequalities.[1]

Our education system is effectively failing 30% of our children. The Education Policy Institute report 2020[2] outlines the following key facts:

- The attainment gap between disadvantaged pupils and their peers has stopped closing for the first time in a decade. Policymakers have not succeeded in responding to earlier reports warning of a major loss of momentum in closing the gap.

- Disadvantaged pupils in England are 18.1 months of learning behind their peers by the time they finish their GCSEs (General Certificate Secondary Educations) – the same gap as five years ago.

- The gap at primary school increased for the first time since 2007 – which may signal that the gap is set to widen in the future.

■ The stalling of the gap occurred even before the COVID-19 pandemic had impacted the education system.

■ Researchers have identified the increasing proportion of disadvantaged children in persistent poverty as a contributory cause of the lack of progress with narrowing the disadvantage gap

There are clearly implications for policy that need to be addressed, and no shortage of debate on this subject, but this book isn't about that, sitting back and waiting for change only serves to prevent more generations of children the opportunity to succeed. This book is about looking at what you can do to develop good quality inclusive practice in your setting to support children who are disadvantaged by background, challenge or need. I believe strongly that ensuring children get access to high-quality Early Years education and care does make a difference and where they get a great start to their education journey it can help to overcome disadvantages and support them to succeed at school.

This book is about Early Years, not just preschool, and in line with other countries, it looks at practice regarding children up to the end of key stage 1, 0–7 years.

It is not intended to cover every aspect of inclusion or Early Years education, as that would be a mammoth task; it is more a reflection of my own learning and one that I hope you will find useful to you in your career. It focuses on my journey of discovery of what has worked for me in developing my own Early Years practice (0–7 years) based on my own experience and that of other teachers and practitioners I have been fortunate to work with along the way. Each chapter contains a true story about an event or challenge that made me question my ethos, values and my practice leading me to where I am today. It doesn't contain all the answers to overcoming disadvantage as so much that impacts on a child's life are beyond our control, but I hope you find it useful and that it encourages you to reflect on your own practice. It can be used by anyone involved in Early Education as a springboard for reflecting on and developing your own practice.

The book begins by defining disadvantage and explores some of the ways it can affect a child's education and life chances. The chapters on Vision and Values, Culture and Inclusion should help you to focus on the kind of setting you want to be and how to achieve it, emphasising the importance of a clear identity and how to project that to the wider community.

One of the greatest advantages to a child is for their parents and carers to be involved in their education and the chapter on parent partnerships is packed full of ideas to support you with this. The impact parents and carers have on their child's education is so critical that you will find them mentioned throughout the other chapters as well.

Learning to read is obviously fundamental to education success, and this is an area in which many children not only are heavily disadvantaged before they start school, but also by the systems we use in school. The Ready to Read chapter gives you many examples of how you can overcome this disadvantage so that inequalities in experience are addressed.

The final chapters Children with Additional Needs and Transitions will help you focus in on the individual children in your setting and how to meet their needs.

As you read through the chapters in this book, take some time to reflect on each of the subjects covered. There are ideas to help you develop your practice at the end of each chapter, these are not exhaustive – they are just ideas, not everything will suit your context and other things may occur to you. The whole purpose is to help you reflect and review and change your practice where you feel it is beneficial to do so; it is not a 'to do' list.

So where am I today? Still learning, and I hope you are too as we will continue to need teachers and practitioners that reflect and refine their practice to meet the needs of the children and young people who are disadvantaged and struggle in education. I always felt privileged to have the opportunity to connect with children and families right at the start of their educational journey, and I have learned that what you do can make a real difference to their future. You have that opportunity too!

Notes

1 UNICEF, 2020, Education and COVID-19.
2 Education Policy Institute, 2020, Education in England Annual Report.

1 | What Is Disadvantage?.

SHEEP, PIGS AND FROGS

Early on in my teaching career I did some supply work and found myself working in a Y3 class with seven and eight year olds and I was accompanying them on a visit to a local farm. There was the usual excitement and noise, and it was clear that for some of these children it was a really big event – some said they had never been on a coach before and others chatted about what they might see at the farm. One boy – Joe, was very quiet and stayed close to me, I had been made aware that he was a 'slow learner', so I decided to sit with him and try to get to know him a bit more. I asked if he had been to a farm and he shook his head, and as he stared out of the window we talked about the things he could see. I could tell he hadn't been very far away from home before, especially when we drove over the bridge about two miles from school and suddenly his eyes widened as he shouted, 'I've seen this on the telly'.

By the time we arrived at the farm he was animated with excitement, they all were, and the first animals we saw were the sheep. The farmer came to meet us and said he was rounding up the sheep for shearing – a great educational opportunity for us so we went to watch. It was at that point that Joe shouted and pointed –

'look Miss there's a sheep over there with no hair on!'

My heart sank as I said the words 'no Joe that's a pig'. I was really shocked – how could a child get to seven years of age and not know what a pig looked like? How small had his world been that he had never learnt to recognise basic farm animals? To me it summed up disadvantage, this boy went nowhere and did very little and was nevertheless expected to be able to make sense of the world in the same way as others who took trips like this for granted.

DOI: 10.4324/9781003016465-2

Looking back this was really a pivotal moment for me, as from then on I made every effort to 'keep it real' – with as many first-hand experiences planned in for children as possible, it became a personal challenge and one I thoroughly enjoyed trying to meet. It was at this point that I stopped planning meaningless activities – for example, cut and stick, or worksheets that did little more than keep children busy. All topics that were planned had to have some kind of real experience as a starting point and as many hands-on purposeful activities as possible. The vocabulary that developed from these experiences was really encouraging and the children seemed really engaged; undoubtedly this was one of the best decisions of my career – it really did make a difference, especially for children who had limited life experiences.

It wasn't all plain sailing though; once when studying the life cycle of a frog we hit trouble. I previously taught this by developing a life cycle wheel with pictures for children to colour in of the various stages – frogspawn, tadpole, froglet and frog – but of course we weren't going to do that now so I collected frog spawn and had a tank in the classroom for children to watch as they developed and they could record what they could see happening. Of course, young children are curious, that's what makes them so exciting to teach, and so I shouldn't have been surprised when one day a small child reached up to the tank and pulled it over. The screams as she was drenched in water were horrendous, as was the hysteria which quickly spread across the classroom, but this was in no way as bad as me having to spend the next half an hour trying to scoop up frogspawn and tadpoles from the carpet and put them back in the tank, convinced somehow that I would be prosecuted under some animal rights law for murdering tadpoles. It still haunts me.

What is disadvantage?

Disadvantage in education terms 'encompasses not only income poverty, but also a lack of social and cultural capital and control over decisions that affect life' (Crenna-Jenkins, 2018).[1] It describes the children that are unable to benefit from the full opportunities that the education system can offer because of a variety of barriers that prevent them from doing so and have a detrimental effect on their outcomes. These disadvantages can be due to a wide variety of complex issues including poverty, the impact of disability or health issues, or as a result of trauma through neglect, abuse or abrupt changes in circumstances.

Children can be disadvantaged due to a number of cultural and societal barriers – gender, ethnic minorities, EAL, Gypsy/Roma/Traveller families, children in care, children with emotional and social development difficulties, children who have no play skills to name a few. This chapter outlines the need for children who are disadvantaged in some way to be given something additional and different to the others, an approach that works to identify the barriers, and practice that goes some way to mitigating the risks that they pose on that child's future – in short it is an individual approach that works to overcome disadvantage.

In England, disadvantage in education is measured by those eligible for free school meals and Pupil Premium funding although this can often hide the true figures as these are reliant on parents registering and not all parents are willing to do this. The relationship between disadvantage and attainment is well documented in the UK and the data clearly shows that children eligible for the Pupil Premium start school behind their better off peers and the gap widens as they go through school.

'Progress is beginning to stall in tackling inequalities in our education system. If current 5 years trends continue, it would take over 500 years for the overall disadvantage gap to close by the end of secondary school' (Fair education alliance, 2019).[2]

Disadvantage and the brain

If we are going to tackle disadvantage we need to start early. As soon as a child is conceived, a wide variety of factors related to poverty and disadvantage come into play which affect the health and well-being of the child. Maternal stress levels and poor nutrition can adversely affect a child's brain development even before birth.

Once a child is born, brain development is rapid, especially in the first three years of life but healthy brain development is dependent on a nurturing environment and stress in the Early Years can have a long-term effect on the architecture of the developing brain.

> Impoverished children have less access to medical care, increased exposure to toxins, violence and income inequality. Having to deal with all of these factors is more than any one person can deal with. It's stressful, and subsequently affecting developmental growth.
>
> (Pollak, 2016)[3]

The development of the amygdala and hippocampus brain regions that support learning, memory, mood and stress reactivity is suppressed in disadvantaged children (Brody et al., 2017), so it is not hard to understand why brain development and educational achievement are linked, why some children struggle to learn and how this adversely affects their life chances.

Attachment

Attachment is like an invisible thread linking the baby and the young child to the significant adults in their life. It is a major aspect of early childhood development and forming secure attachments and is vital for good emotional development. It is from these emotional bonds that the child gains security, becomes resilient and able to form positive relationships with others. The relationships young children form act as a blueprint for their future relationships and learning, so it is important to get it right from the start as this is key to closing the disadvantage gap. All Early Years settings should not only be aware of Attachment but should have active processes for developing secure attachments with children as well as recognising where a child may have poor attachments outside of the setting.

> If broken attachments and serial carers are to be the norm then we are disregarding all we know about the importance of stable, healthy, secure relationships with just a few special people to nurture children's wellbeing, health and dispositions for learning.
>
> Dorothy Y. Selleck[4]

Babies are completely dependent for everything on their principle carer. As they try to make sense of the way their world works it is the reciprocal relationships and the unconditional love and care they receive that makes this possible. They soon become attached to their main carer in a special way. Steve Biddulph (Biddulph, n.d.)[5] in his book 'raising boys' comments on the difference between our culture and what he calls wiser cultures and how they form strong attachments with their children. One Balinese tradition is the first 'setting down to earth' of a new baby does not take place until the child is six months old. Before this the child is never out of someone's arms or in a sling; it is obvious that this culture values attachment highly. The meeting of basic physical needs, and building a sense of personal security, forms the bedrock of intellectual, social, emotional and physical development. This idea is central to the theories of the developmental psychologist Maslow, first proposed in 1943, and still very relevant today.

Maslow[6] stated that people are instinctively motivated to achieve certain needs. When one need is fulfilled a person seeks to fulfil the next one, and so on.

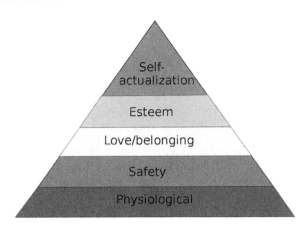

Figure 1.1 Maslow's hierarchy of needs.

This is why his model is often depicted as a pyramid. Maslow's Pyramid (Figure 1.1) shows that the degree of 'self-actualisation', that is, being a strong resilient capable learner will not happen if basic needs remain unfulfilled.

The role of the key person

The key person is a designated person who takes on a very special responsibility for individual children in the setting while those on whom the child usually depends are not there. The key person approach in all settings makes a massive difference to children and parents when it is well planned and thoughtfully implemented and is key to understanding the barriers that are preventing children from learning. The key person finds out all about the child, helps them to settle when they first start and works out with the parents their individual settling in procedures that will best suit the child. In a setting the key person forms the strongest relationship between the setting, child and family.

> Each child *must* be assigned a key person. Their role is to help ensure that every child's care is tailored to meet their individual needs, to help the child become familiar with the setting, offer a settled relationship for the child and build a relationship with their parents.
> Statutory Framework for the Early Years Foundation Stage. Page 21. 3.27

The Early Years Foundation Stage (EYFS) acknowledges this very important role that practitioners have to play. It has become a statutory requirement because ensuring children's emotional security is paramount to a child's well-being.

Coupled with this is an important neuro-scientific fact: *an anxious brain will not learn!*

'The key person makes sure that, within the day-to day demands of the setting each child feels individual, cherished and thought about by someone in particular while they are away from home'.[7]

Early Years Pupil Premium

The UK government's answer to closing the disadvantage gap is to provide additional funding for pupils in schools who are disadvantaged in the form of pupil premium and followed it up with Early Years Pupil Premium (EYPP) funding in 2015. EYPP is given to providers of Early Years education to support their most disadvantaged three and four year olds. This was a long time coming, since Pupil Premium in schools was introduced in 2011, and was warmly welcomed by the Early Years sector, as it went some way towards the recognition that disadvantage does not start at the school gate and there is much that can be done in early education to ensure better outcomes for those most at risk. It says something about our education system if Early Years is the last place to receive funding and that funding equates to only an additional 53p per hour compared with £1,345 per annum for children in primary school, and an even greater amount for looked after children. Indeed, most interventions to close the gap are funded at school level, but surely if we started to address the issues much earlier there would be less need later on.

A 2017 DfE report showed that although many settings were getting used to the process and finding it easier to navigate the system, they still reported that it remained a challenge to be able to evidence the spend against outcomes:

> …there was broad consensus that providers would welcome additional support and guidance to monitor spending and assess effectiveness, including at a more strategic level and across settings.[8]

To meet growing demand and to capitilise on opportunity, a wide variety of resources and services have popped up on the market that support the spending of the EYPP, but this can have the effect of adding to the dilemma surrounding decision making, as they all claim to be the answer, but how do you address the key issue – how do you really know what you need?

A survey[9] undertaken by the Department for Education (DFE) found that the funding was commonly used to provide targeted support for individual children, to pay for literacy and numeracy resources, to support staff development and purchase outdoor resources. The report also outlines that the group-based providers, that is, those outside of the maintained sector, were more likely to use the funding to benefit all the children in the setting (60%) and the highest expected impact reported (28%) was that it would raise the quality for all children in the setting.

Anything that supports raising quality and providing better resources is undoubtedly good news, but the EYPP needs to go further than this if it is really going to fulfil its core purpose of reducing inequality between children from lower-income families and their better off peers.

The Social Mobility Commission's[10] State of the Nation report in 2016 warns that Britain's deep social mobility problem is getting worse. It reports that children in deprived areas are twice as likely to be in childcare that is not good enough, compared with the most prosperous areas and recommends the Government double EYPP funding as part of an overall strategy to raise quality. This raises the issue for the whole sector that greater investment is needed in order to drive up quality by ensuring the profession is highly valued and it is an attractive option for those who are interested in pursuing a career in early education. This will only happen if the sector can attract and retain qualified practitioners and it is hard to see how the EYPP is going to be able to drive that agenda in its current form.

So how do you use the EYPP to raise quality and improve outcomes for disadvantaged children?

The starting point must be the child, working out what they need, and developing a clear understanding of what you want to achieve. This can only be done by building a strong relationship with the parents/carers so you have a clear picture of the child, understand fully the context and dynamics of the family unit so you can develop a joined up approach to meeting the child's needs. Practitioners need to develop strong learning partnerships with parents so that they are able to support their children with their next steps in learning (see Chapter 5). This approach is key to supporting children who are disadvantaged; you need to fully understand their context and the environment that they come from. Relationships with parents will help you understand the kinds of experiences children have had before they enter your setting and what you may need to provide for them in order to support their development. For example, if a child has had limited outdoor experiences, their physical skills may need developing and exploring the outdoors will be a significant element in the plans for that child.

Recent years have seen many teachers and practitioners leaving the profession, citing workload as an issue. At last there is a move away from a data-driven culture, with targets and next steps for every child often being cited as the cause of excessive workload in Early Years. The new Education Inspection Framework (Ofsted, 2019)[11] and the new EYFS framework (2021) do address this by making it clear that you do not have to provide masses of data for every child and that more time should be spent interacting with children than observing them. However, some children particularly ones from disadvantaged backgrounds do still need to have their progress tracked carefully so that practitioners are really armed with the knowledge they need in order to improve the outcomes for the children eligible for EYPP, supporting them to make informed choices, now and in the future about how to spend the money to improve outcomes. It may be that one child has a specific need, or that there is a trend emerging in the data, for example several children who have some kind of communication or language difficulty may highlight the need for whole setting training in best practice in this area. Starting from the needs of the child and considering the training needs of the staff will positively support the decision-making process.

Another area that is often overlooked is how will the impact of any intervention will be monitored; it is essential that you know from the start what you are trying to achieve and then you monitor progress carefully. This child–centred approach is much more likely to have an impact than the setting centred approach of deciding what equipment or resources are needed, or, the often random, choices from toolkits or websites.

However, even where the spending is being used to really good effect, challenges remain. Currently, settings receive approximately £300 per year for each eligible three– and four-year-old. This compares to £1,345 for pupils in reception to Year 6. It is easy to see that this very small amount of funding makes the decisions about spending even more difficult as there is unlikely to be sufficient funding to benefit from economies of scale.

If you add in the fact that there may only be a handful of eligible children in the setting and the issue that children remain in the setting for a very short period of time, it can feel almost impossible to make long–term strategic decisions around the best use of funding, and it is easy to see why settings are inclined to spend the money to have an enduring impact and to benefit the maximum number of children.

As the sector continues to struggle to meet its ongoing costs, it is easy to see how these practical issues conspire against being able to plan strategically, often leading to impulsive spending. To put that into context, the survey reports that group-based providers had received on average £1,157 EYPP funding in the last 12 months. 'Close to half (47%) received less than £1,000 and less than one in four (23%) received £1,000 or more'.[12] There is also little doubt that some settings are not always in receipt of the full funding due to a reluctance for some parents to disclose their details or a lack of confidence in approaching parents to discuss their personal circumstances. More training around how to build effective partnerships with parents and a less bureaucratic system is definitely needed.

To add to what is currently quite a confusing system, EYPP is only payable for children who meet the criteria from three years of age. Children who are considered to be vulnerable or disadvantaged at two are eligible for 15 hours funded childcare, but not EYPP. This is because the hourly rate paid to settings for two year olds is higher than that paid for the three and four year olds, and the rationale is that it is already 'built in'. This is a flawed argument as the additional funding barely meets the costs that the higher staff ratios; the EYFS states that there should be one adult for every four children aged two, but only one adult for every eight children aged three and over; yet the funding is only approximately 15% higher than that paid for three and four year olds. There is also the issue that the criteria for two-year-old funding and EYPP are slightly different, so some children become eligible for EYPP when they turn three and some do not and this also changes on a termly basis. This disjointed and complicated funding system creates unnecessary administrative processes and fails to address the need for settings to be able to make long-term strategic plans, and more importantly meet the ongoing needs of the child. It would be so much simpler to operate a system where any child deemed disadvantaged enough to qualify for a funded place at two was automatically entitled to EYPP for the whole of their time in the setting. The extra cost of implementing this system would undoubtedly be at least partly balanced by the reduction in the complex and confusing administrative systems that are inherent in the existing process.

Providers say that the EYPP is making a difference to disadvantaged children, but only where the decisions around spending are made in the full knowledge of the needs of the child and it is linked to clearly stated desired outcomes. The EYPP is reported to be making some difference to disadvantaged children, but often that is short term and difficult to evidence and it is more widely reported to be benefiting whole setting improvements. This is largely because the current system is underfunded, short term, disjointed and often confusing to administer. The funding is clearly insufficient and the barriers that conspire against a strategic approach to spending need to be removed. Only then will we begin to see an increase in the use of EYPP to impact on outcomes for individual children, where the decisions around spending are made in the full knowledge of the needs of the child and funding can be predicted on a longer term basis to enable this to happen.

Cultural capital

Another example of the government's approach to tackling disadvantage was to introduce cultural capital in the new Education Inspection Framework (2019).

Listening to two Early Years practitioners talking in a setting, I overheard one say 'they expect us to do so much and now we have to *do* cultural capital'. To which the other one responded 'no we'll be fine we've got the music CDs for that'.

It made me smile, but it raises a serious point – how do you '*do* cultural capital'? It's hardly surprising that the term is misunderstood, as it is a new term in Early Years education and is arguably open to interpretation.

To answer this question fully we need to look at the history and intent behind the terminology. Pierre Bourdieu was the first to define cultural capital[13] and he talked about it in terms of assets, speech, accent, education and hobbies and interests. He noted that children from disadvantaged backgrounds were, on the whole, achieving less at school and had poorer access to cultural opportunities, which, in turn, affected social mobility, well-being and life outcomes. In short, he argues culture is a class issue. This fits in with the government's intention to reduce social inequalities and ensure all children have access to the same life opportunities. We all know that some children have parents who are constantly topping up their cultural capital – they go on family trips, visit libraries, access sports and clubs and have access to a wide variety of cultural experiences. This is not the case for other children who live very differently and have limited access to experiences beyond the immediate ones that are part of daily life.

Liz Brooker[14] describes this as the difference between the 'national' curriculum and the 'natural' curriculum that is offered by families. It is easy to see how children who have had many experiences in their Early Years have more 'hooks' to hang their new knowledge on when they come into school – a greater existing cultural capital, which offers them a distinct advantage over the others. Some practitioners are struggling to see how cultural capital fits in with their practice and concerns are expressed around what the inspectors will expect to see and hear in relation to this. But there is no need to plan for it separately as it should seamlessly link to and extend your daily practice. As far as Ofsted is concerned you just need to be able to explain why you have chosen your activities and how they link to and extend the child's learning and development. In an Early Years setting, cultural capital means that each child arrives with a number of experiences, knowledge and ideas based on their own personal circumstances, all of which is valid and should be respected. Early Years providers should be confident that they are able to demonstrate their knowledge of the child and family context and show their provision builds on this, by deepening and widening their experiences and knowledge. This needs to involve showing the children the 'awe and wonder' of the world, so that they become enthusiastic, motivated and engaged learners. In order to do this you need to know about the home life and the context they live in and build out from there; developing strong parental partnerships is key to this as is taking the time to understand their culture and valuing their role.

Reflecting on your own cultural capital can be helpful here; considering your own familial norms and understanding how they influenced you provide a useful lens to consider what do children bring to the setting in terms of their existing capital and how can you extend their experiences from this.

It is important to remember that Early Years practice is usually based around the children's interests and their existing knowledge and experience – developing cultural capital is no different – it is about extending the child's world one experience at a time. Every child is unique, and that they learn and develop in different ways and the experiences that we provide for children need to be relevant to their learning and be culturally and developmentally appropriate. It is not about choosing cultural activities for their own sake – 'cultural capital' activities such as visiting galleries or museums will mean little to the child unless of course they link to their interests; rather it is about taking the time to choose activities that extend the child's world and enthuse and motivate them to learn and preparing them for what comes next. Exploring and celebrating the different cultures and experiences of the children and families in your setting is an ideal way to extend children's knowledge of the world, so you don't need to go far to find rich and diverse experiences for children to learn from. In short, cultural capital is not new; it is basically just good, child-centred Early Years practice.

Top tips for developing cultural capital

- A good understanding of the local area is helpful, what is within walking distance that you can visit? Where does the bus go? What is of specific interest nearby?

- Rather than looking for hidden meaning in the phrase, practitioners should continue to focus on giving each child the best start in life and the support that enables them to fulfil their full potential.

- Really get to know the family and gain an understanding of the context the child lives in.

- Plan as many real-life experiences as possible – going to the shops to buy ingredients for baking, taking a bus or train to visit local places of interest that link it to the learning or visit the library to choose books that link to areas of interest. Developing vocabulary starts with having something to talk about.

■ Understand the child's culture and important events in their life and plan activities around that for others to share and understand.

■ Listening to relaxing music at nap time.

■ Take the time to 'smell the roses' and walk on the grass barefoot – one of the best things about Early Years practice is being able to really focus on simple activities that bring out the awe and wonder factor!

■ Use the 'capital' your parents and staff bring – get them to share their culture, knowledge and skills. The following case study demonstrates how one setting did just this to develop the knowledge and skills of the children and how they used it as a hook for learning.

CASE STUDY – BRICKS AND BRIDGES

Sunny attends nursery three days a week and is captivated by the large bricks. He is always building bridges. The key person talked to mum who explained that Sunny's dad is a construction worker and builds and restores bridges – the practitioner asked if dad could visit and bring some pictures of his bridges in for the children to see. Sunny's dad provided lots of pictures and Sunny spoke about them to the other children. This created an enthusiasm for bridges and many children were enthused and excited to build them in the block area and talk about them happily. The practitioners took children to see local bridges – a railway bridge, a footbridge and a road bridge over a river. They discussed why you needed bridges, what they were for and why they were important. They provided books with pictures of bridges and read the children 'The Three Billy Goats Gruff' and the story of 'Pooh Sticks'. Luckily there was a park nearby where they could play 'Pooh sticks' and the school playground had a bridge so they could act out and retell the stories for themselves.

Disadvantage is not necessarily a predeterminer of outcomes, almost everyone can point to someone who, despite significant disadvantage, went on to be successful. But in almost every case you think of where someone has done well there will be someone there with them who made the effort to support that person to overcome their challenges. You can overcome the effect of disadvantage if you first recognise what it is and how it impacts on children and then work to find solutions. Recognising that a child is in some way disadvantaged is only the first step; it's what you do about it that makes the difference.

Reviewing and developing practice

- Ensure your key person system is well thought out and centres on developing a strong relationship with the child and family.

- Have a robust admission and settling in policy during which time the key person gets to know the family and child (see chapter on parental engagement).

- Ensure physical needs are well catered for, food, drink, sleep and personal care.

- Plan as many real-life first-hand experiences as you can – this will develop children's vocabulary and build and extend their understanding of the world around them – building their cultural capital.

- Ensure staff are all fully aware of child development and always start from where the child is developmentally, not just how old they are. Know your parents and your children really well, understand their context and environment – where might you have to widen their experiences? How can you support their involvement?

- Build strong supportive relationships with parents so conversations about signing up for EYPP are part of this approach.

- Identify need – individually and in terms of trends across all the children.

- Consider EYPP spending in terms of existing resources and staff knowledge and expertise – where are the gaps? Would the staff benefit from additional training?

- Know what you want the impact of your EYPP spend to be and how you will monitor it.

Notes

1 Crenna-Jenkins, W. (2018). Key drivers of the disadvantage gap – literature review. EPI.
2 Fair education alliance (2019) *Education in England Annual Report 2019*.
3 Pollack, S. (2016). How living in poverty affects children's brain development. Accessed online: https://today.duke.edu/2016/10/how-living-poverty-affects-children%E2%80%99s-brain-development.
4 Selleck, D.Y., in Why attachment matters, Primed for lIfe, 2016.
5 Biddulph, S. (n.d.). *Raising Boys*.

6   Maslow, A. H. (1943). A theory of human motivation. *Psychological Review, 50*(4), 370–396.

7   Elfer, P. (2002). Attachment and the key person role.

8   DfE (2017). Study of Early Education and Development: Experiences of the Early Years Pupil Premium.

9   Dfe (2017). Early Years Pupil Premium: providers survey, Research Report.

10 Social Mobility Commission (2016) State of the Nation 2016: Social Mobility in Great Britain.

11 Osted (2019) The Education Inspection Framework. Available at: https://assets.publishing. service.gov.uk/government/uploads/system/uploads/attachment_data/file/801429/ Education_inspection_framework.pdf (accessed 20.6.2020).

12 McGinigal, S., Panayiotou, S., Fahliogullari, S., Witsø, C., Cordes, A., Harrison, M. (2017). *Early Years Pupil Premium: Providers Survey Research report January 2017*. Kantar Public, p. 7.

13 Bourfieu, P., and Patterson, J. C. Cultural Reproduction and Social Reproduction.

14 Brooker, L. (2015). 'Cultural Capital in the Preschool Years: Can the state "compensate" for the family?' in Alenen, L., Brooker, L., and Mayall, B. (eds.) *Childhood with Bourdieu*. Cambridge: Palgrave McMillan.

2 The Culture of Early Years

PACKAWAY HEROES

When I was on maternity leave, I got involved with the local preschool. It was set up in the parish hall, just across from the school. Each morning I would go in and help them pull everything out from under the stage, you had to bend to get in and out and everything was packed in tightly, so you had to be fit and strong. You then had to set it all up, create zones, mix paint and get things ready. It took three people about 45 minutes of hard work to get it done. The children would come in for three hours and when they had gone you had to pack away; this was even harder than setting up as there was cleaning and sweeping to be done. At about 1 pm, after almost five hours of hard work we were done, it was absolutely exhausting, but we did it as there was no other preschool provision close by and we wanted our own children and those of the community to benefit. The pay was poor, but at least by 1 pm you had the rest of the day to yourself, there were no observations, no planning to be done, in fact no paperwork at all, it really was just about play in those days.

Compare that to now when there is so much bureaucracy in early education and so many more things to think about and plan, all done outside the sessions. Yet, pack away preschools still exist, run by people on low pay who are totally committed to the children and families, and you would have to say in poor working conditions. These people are amazing – I take my hat off to them!

DOI: 10.4324/9781003016465-3

What is early education?

The Early Years sector is complex and varied and often misunderstood as a result. Unlike other education sectors, the Early Years Foundation Stage (EYFS) is delivered in a variety of settings including schools, village halls, nurseries, children's centres and even childminders' own homes. It suffers from an identity crisis as many people are unclear about its purpose; is it education or is it childcare? If a child attends a day nursery is that childcare? Or if they go to a school-based setting is that education? This confusion is further compounded by the different levels of qualifications; maybe it is only qualified teachers that offer education? and of course, the deeply rooted perception that children under five are 'just playing'.

This confusion stems from its history; nursery schools were first set up during the first world war as more mothers needed to work, but the hardships that followed in the subsequent years saw more nurseries set up as a way of overcoming deprivation. These nurseries focused mainly on meeting physical needs, such as nutrition, and were seen as a safe space for children to eat, rest and grow. The education act 1944[1] did show some intention to make nursery provision a universal service but it never happened. It wasn't until 1960 when the Pre-school Playgroup movement was formed that preschool provision started to expand. The sector grew as more and more preschools were set up, often run by volunteers and paid for by the parents. They were social spaces for children, and only if parents could afford it could their children attend, and they were often only used by parents who stayed at home as they had limited opening hours. As more and more women went out to work the need for childcare increased and day nurseries were set up and more people registered to be childminders; these were childcare solutions for working parents, very little was ever said about early education.

The childcare act (2006)[2] saw the development of the EYFS framework for learning, development and care for children from birth to five. It was the first time the sector had any kind of standards framework that covered the whole age range and was seen as a way of developing quality and consistency across all provision. The EYFS framework[3] became statutory in 2008 and has undergone reviews since then but not really moved away from its core themes and principles, early learning had arrived. However, culturally the EYFS has had a hard job of shaking off its childcare and preschool play image. The EYFS is not a statutory phase, children do not have to attend, and it is sometimes viewed as less important than school, as it is perceived that is where 'real learning' starts. The sector struggles for funding, wages are low and qualification levels much lower than what is needed to teach in school.

All of this has contributed to a culture where often early years is often viewed as a stepping stone to school, somewhere children go to play and socialise or a facility for working parents.

Learning and play

Ofsted makes the case that 'Research has never been clearer – a child's early education lasts a lifetime. Securing a successful start for our youngest children, and particularly those from disadvantaged backgrounds, is crucial'.[4]

Early years education is, therefore, important and is enshrined in legislation, but even the statutory requirements give the impression that the early years sector is about preparing for something else, 'school readiness'.

The EYFS Framework 'promotes teaching and learning to ensure children's "school readiness" and gives children the broad range of knowledge and skills that provide the right foundation for good future progress through school and life'.

Real learning is often not associated with the EYFS, being perceived by some to start in Key Stage 1 and is typically defined by a child sitting with a pencil in their hand, or on a carpet with an adult talking to them. Indeed most policy makers have this memory of what education was like for them and so they want to see it replicated, so how can we ensure that learning in the EYFS is valued and what principles can we take from the pedagogy?

If we start by looking at teaching and learning and explore what those terms mean, learning in the EYFS becomes clearer. In its simplest form, teaching is about enabling learning and good teaching is about using the best method to make that learning happen. Learning is about the acquisition of a new piece of knowledge or skill and effective learning links to prior knowledge or skills and enables the child to apply the learning in context.

In Early Years, it looks to the untrained eye as though children are 'just playing'. Play is a crucial element in good Early Years practice, but if you look carefully you will see the child learning and practising new skills, extending their vocabulary, exploring and testing themselves and the world around them, developing socially, learning societal and cultural norms, expressing their needs and developing self-confidence. When you consider all this, it certainly looks like 'real work'; indeed to the child there is no distinction between play and learning. So, what about teaching? In early years settings, the adult plays a crucial role in their interactions with children at play using careful questioning techniques to promote discussion and encourage further exploration as well as providing the resources needed for children's next steps in their learning. This requires accurate assessment of children's developmental stage and using their knowledge of child development to assess whether this was within typical development parameters or that the child may need extra support. Planning is centred around what the child can do and what their next steps in learning are, usually incorporating the child's interests and catering for their specific needs. Activities can be wholly or partially child or adult led and may gradually move towards more formal teaching, but it is not a straight line of progression as different desired outcomes require different methodology. This is highly skilled work as decisions need to be made on the spot about what each individual child needs next, including when to intervene and when to stand back, when to instruct and when to follow the child's lead, and yet we often hear it referred to as 'only play'.

Moving into Key Stage I

This pedagogy is central to the EYFS because it considers the holistic needs of the child and their age and stage of development. It does not separate play from learning, as for young children play is learning. Very few countries move away from this play-based pedagogy as early as we do in the UK, with many children not starting formal learning until they are 6 or 7, but a child of just 60 months can enter Key Stage 1 in a UK school and this can cause issues if it is not carefully managed.

'Child development tells us that children's learning needs in Year 1 are broadly similar to those for children in the Reception year and that children should not go from being seen as a "unique child" to a "Year 1" in one small step down the corridor'.[5]

So why is Key Stage 1 so different to the EYFS in some schools? There are many good reasons why it becomes more difficult to have a play-based pedagogy in Year 1: ratios may be higher, there is more pressure to fill books with work so that progress can be evidenced, a change to the curriculum and the looming pressure of tests, etc. but for many children this sudden abrupt change in the way they are expected to engage with their learning is difficult to adjust to and can cause a dip in progress as a result. Effective transition needs to be a smooth and gradual process, that builds on and extends what has gone before and, as the pedagogical approach in the EYFS is often quite different to that in Key Stage 1, developing a shared understanding amongst staff is surely the first step. The chapter on transitions explores this in more detail.

Planning also needs careful consideration; it is all too easy to fall into a default mode of teaching, a comfort zone, where the style and method of delivery is dictated by the preference of the adult, or the subject norms instead of the needs of the child. Young children need a range of styles and methods from informal and wholly child initiated, to very formal and wholly adult initiated; the important thing is that the best method is used for the desired outcome and the age and stage of development of the child is considered.

For example, you sometimes see very young children sitting on the carpet for extended periods of time with phonic flashcards; this fits well with the idea that phonics is 'real learning' and the pressure is on for children to pass their phonics check in Year 1 – so it needs to be done. Or does it? Is there another way? Consider the teacher who uses the outside space as a resource for learning, or the sand or water tray for children to fish out words and digraphs, or chalk to practice writing, or hoops with letters in to collect objects. An interactive, multisensory engaging lesson achieves the desired objective, and takes into consideration the age and stage of the child. It can be extended easily, if the children show signs that they are ready to move on. This is a recognised approach in Reception, but often does not continue into Year 1, sometimes due to a lack of understanding of play-based learning and Early Years pedagogy.

Play in school is often viewed as something children do when they have finished their 'real work', a treat or a chance to let off steam so that they can concentrate better afterwards. It is even withdrawn on occasions, as a punishment for 'bad behaviour' or not working hard enough to complete set tasks. Sometimes teachers set aside special times for play as a treat for working hard, often called 'Golden Time', which sends a clear message that play is a reward for hard work, and that real work is always adult initiated.

Most schools have teacher-led classrooms once the children move into Key Stage 1, and plan dedicated teaching times for teaching communication, language and literacy, and this is usually done with rigour. The teaching can become activity focused, sometimes centering around worksheets, cutting and sticking activities and other tasks designed and planned by the teacher, some of which do little to motivate and extend the learning. Real learning, however, comes from when the children have the opportunity to practise their skills and apply their learning to different contexts and it is this time that is often squeezed out in the classroom, as more and more teaching is timetabled in. As adults, we must learn new things all the time, new skills at work, new hobbies and skills for everyday life. Rarely is that learning truly embedded if we don't see the point and how it links to something we know already, and without practice we often quickly forget. Children are no different, but it is not that uncommon to find schools that timetable teacher-led activities throughout the day, with no opportunity for children to make choices about how to practise and extend their learning.

A teacher-led classroom can also lead to diminished opportunities for children to develop their speaking skills. Without doubt the ability to speak well in a variety of contexts using a rich and wide vocabulary paves the way for success at reading and writing and arguably even to leading successful adult lives. Some schools employ methods such as 'talk for writing' which are successful, but do we need to go further? What about 'talk for learning'? Talking about concepts, questioning and explaining your thinking are key for the development of high-order learning and need daily practice. Just how much time is planned for children to question each other, discuss concepts, explain their methods, challenge each other's thinking in the average classroom? It would be interesting to see how much talking is planned for in the school day.

In England, we have a National Curriculum which is knowledge-based, that means the content requires children to remember important subject information and they are then tested on that knowledge periodically. There is much debate as to the pros and cons of this approach, but I believe a key problem with a knowledge-based curriculum is that it encourages a timetabled approach and an overemphasis on schemes of work. If learning is to be meaningful it should be to meet a need, to solve a problem or satisfy a curiosity and its purpose needs to be clear. Not many of us undertake learning for its own sake; we need a reason to attend a class or do a piece of research either to solve a problem, or to open a future opportunity, but all too often young children are taught to do things without the purpose being clearly explained or shown.

The teaching of Mathematics is a good example of this; children are often taught skills out of context in line with a scheme of work and then have limited opportunity to apply their skills. Adults set up Maths corners with weighing tables, or give out worksheets with lines to measure, or ask children to sort shapes or count their faces or recognise coins. Why? What is it for? What does it mean to the children? And more importantly when the lesson is over how or when will they practice using their skills? Surely it is better to teach children the skills they need in order to do something else and making sure all opportunities are used – measuring round heads to make headbands, weighing ingredients for cooking, working out how many chairs we will need to put out for assembly, sharing fruit or sweets for fractions, adding up scores for the game of skittles, buying things in the shop, making sure each class gets the right number of pieces of fruit, referring to time and the clock throughout the day, etc. Often these are activities that just get overlooked as learning opportunities in the rush to get back to the planned formal learning, but they give context and purpose and allow children to develop their skills and understanding, and therefore embed their learning. Children who have had limited experiences before they start school have fewer 'hooks' on which to hang new learning. If they cannot connect the learning to something else they may not fully grasp it. For example, in the National Curriculum[6] Key Stage 1 Science talks about identifying trees and the structure of flowers, very easy for the child who has a garden, is taken to the park or has an adult that has supported them through many discussions about nature and the seasons. But for the child who has had limited experiences this may not make sense as so often Key Stage 1 learning is done inside the classroom.

The pedagogy in the EYFS is designed to make children curious, support them to grow and develop a thirst for learning. It has the characteristics of effective teaching and learning clearly embedded in it:

- Playing and exploring – children investigate and experience things, and 'have a go'

- Active learning – children concentrate and keep on trying if they encounter difficulties, and enjoy achievements

- Creating and thinking critically – children have and develop their own ideas, make links between ideas and develop strategies for doing things[7]

The UK is one of only a handful of countries that leave this behind before a child's sixth birthday. Why if it is recognised as effective would you stop teaching in this way? Looking at these characteristics do they not apply to all learning at any age?

It is time the EYFS had the recognition it deserves and that the way it operates is fundamental to good child development and builds strong foundations for learning. Once this is recognised, maybe it will have a higher status in our culture and our education system would not be in such as hurry to leave its principles and practice behind.

Development of practice

- Ensure you fully understand the principles of the EYFS and why they are beneficial to children's learning.

- Observe children and look for where and when you see the characteristics of effective teaching and learning taking place – discuss as a team.

- Brush up on your child development so you can talk confidently about what children need to support their next steps in learning.

- Look at the National Curriculum – what experiences do children need to have had to fully access it? Consider which children will be disadvantaged when they get there and build in as many real-life experiences for them as you can.

- Be an active campaigner for EY practice and be able to articulate the children's learning to anyone that asks you about it or puts pressure on you to change your practice, for example, can you talk about how painting on an easel links to writing or how playing with small world resources foster creativity?

- Look at practice and pedagogy in Key Stage 1 – does it follow seamlessly on from the EYFS? Which areas could be aligned better? How could you take this forward?

Notes

1 Education Act 1944 (2015) Retrieved 3 May 2020, from http://www.legislation.gov.uk/ukpga/Geo6/7–8/31/section/8/enacted

2 The Stationery OYce Limited under the authority and superintendence of Carol Tullo, Controller of Her Majesty's Stationery OYce and Queen's Printer of Acts of Parliament (2016) *childcare act 2006* [Ebook] UK. Retrieved from http://www.legislation.gov.uk/ukpga/2006/21/pdfs/ukpga_20060021_en.pdf

3 Department for Education (2017) *Statutory Framework for the Early Years Foundation Stage.* Available at: https://www.gov.uk/government/publications/early-years-foundation-stage-framework--2 (Accessed: 12 May 2020)

4 Teaching and play in the early years – a balancing act?
Agood practice survey to explore perceptions of teaching and play in the early years, Ofsted 2015.

5 Julie Fisher: Moving on to Key Stage 1.

6 DfE (2013) National Curriculum in England.

7 DfE (2021) Statutory Framework for the Early Years Foundation Stage.

3 Inclusion

MELANIE

Melanie arrived in my Reception class unannounced on the first day of the new September intake. She hadn't attended a playgroup and her parents had not given any information about her to the school other than the briefest of details on the form. As all the other children were settling in, Melanie was crawling round the room under tables and grunting. Her grandmother assured me she would be fine; she had been brought up bilingual and was just unsure of which language to use. That was her parting comment and she quickly left. Other parents began to leave and I was left in sole charge of all these new children, thankfully most just got on and played, but some were crying and needed comforting, and then there was Melanie – who was by now rolling around and making animal noises. I did my best to approach her and talk to her, but it was as if she wasn't there – she would not look at me or interact with anyone else. The other children got on and played, even the criers eventually stopped, but Melanie just rolled and grunted. I asked a colleague from the next class to get me some help and the Headteacher arrived about ten minutes later to see the problem. He was a 'no nonsense' kind of man and upon looking at Melanie he went off to make a call; it was to the Educational Psychologist. I struggled through the morning and gave some anxious feedback to her grandmother when she collected her at lunchtime; she was not impressed and told me I had not made the effort that was needed to welcome her. The next day the Educational Psychologist arrived to observe Melanie, who was now beginning to make some effort to use language, but it was clear she was a child with many additional needs. A special school placement was recommended, and Melanie was gone after three days. The speed of this process is hard to believe these days, but this at a time when LA support was at its highest level, long before

DOI: 10.4324/9781003016465-4

the idea of buying in services came along and long before inclusion was even a whisper in school. Things in class were much easier with Melanie gone but I was bothered by the whole thing and remember thinking how I had failed this little girl. There was so little I could do at the time as I had a whole class to teach and spending all my time with one child was impossible. I spoke to the head, and we discussed how we might be better prepared in future; he somewhat reluctantly agreed to me being able to undertake home visits in future so that we could better prepare to meet the needs of children and would at least have met them and their families before they arrived on day one. This started an ongoing quest to ensure I was fully prepared to meet the needs of all children and transition processes were robust enough to make sure that I was never caught out again. I learnt a valuable lesson that only when you fully understand a child's needs can you plan to meet them effectively – sounds obvious doesn't it? I have taught many children with additional needs since and the success has always been down to good communication with parents and effective planning. Poor Melanie, I do wonder what happened to her.

What is inclusion?

Inclusive education is still a relatively new concept and has not fully reached maturity. The education act 1981[1] was the driver that began the move from segregation where children with additional needs or disabilities were taught in special schools, to integration where children attended the same school, but their education was mostly separate from their peers. This has now developed into inclusion, where children with additional needs are meant to be fully included alongside their peers. Inclusion values diversity and the unique contribution every child brings to the setting, so that every child has their needs met and is supported to overcome their challenges. It sounds like common sense and the foundation for a strong and supportive society, so why is it still not happening everywhere and why do we struggle with it?

The word inclusion itself is not always helpful; as it suggests there is a set norm, a mainstream child that is accepted and others who sit outside these parameters. For those children we must make reasonable adjustments, so they can be included as part of the group. It follows, therefore, that if it doesn't work, we can then exclude some children if they are deemed to not fit in with the group in some way, at least we tried! This may be part of the problem as our education system has not developed in line with the idea that all children are not the same and cannot be educated in the same way. Broadly speaking, it is hard to be fully inclusive in an education system that was designed for children that fit into the parameters of 'normal' and we are now working as hard as we can to make inclusive, but it actually requires a fundamental rethink of how and why we do things and the flexibility to bend and change as required.

We need an education system that fits the needs of the individual child, not one that we have to mould the child to fit into. That way every child would be considered unique and the education they receive would be tailored to fit their needs. Is that a pipe dream, or a real possibility if we look at things differently? Further information on how to support children with SEND can be found in Chapter 6.

But inclusion doesn't only apply to children with SEND; it's about belonging and being a part of a community, so it spreads across gender, race and culture as well. In its basic sense it is about recognising and appreciating the uniqueness of every child and their community and culture. Time spent on discussing and celebrating cultural and racial differences will help to break down barriers and being proactive around challenging gender stereotypes will help to prepare children to take their place in a multicultural and diverse world.

My work in Early Years means that inclusion is always at the forefront of my mind, so imagine my surprise when I realised that the word does not appear once in the statutory framework for the Early Years Foundation Stage (EYFS). Reflecting on this was a light bulb moment – you do not need to include children if they are already a part of something!

Two of the four guiding principles in the EYFS state that:

'every child is a **unique child**, who is constantly learning and can be resilient, capable, confident and self-assured'; and '**children develop and learn in different ways and at different rates**. The framework covers the education and care of all children in early years provision, including children with special educational needs and disabilities'.

This underlying philosophy needs to be present throughout all education establishments – you are welcome, and we value you for what you bring, and we will support you to be successful. This would lead to a whole new approach to teaching and learning and what is more the answers are already there – just check out the EYFS framework and take from it the guiding principles and the characteristics of effective learning.

Barriers to inclusion

So, what is stopping this from happening? What are the barriers to fully inclusive practice?

The first barrier is parental perception. Many parents of children with additional needs are unwilling to put their child into an Early Years setting, maybe because they fear the setting will not be able to meet their child's needs or that they will be met with a refusal. Not only does this mean that those children miss out, but also the family may suffer economic disadvantage if they cannot access work due to a lack of childcare.

A Parliamentary Inquiry into Childcare for Disabled Children in 2014[2] found that:

- Only 40% of parent carers believe childcare providers in their area can cater for their child

- Families of disabled children are 2.5 times more likely to have no parent working

- Eighty-three per cent parent carers say lack of suitable childcare is the main barrier to paid work

It is easy to jump to the conclusion that parents are protective of their child and feel that only they can meet their needs, but in fact behind these statistics are many stories where parents have approached a local setting and have either met with a flat refusal to take their child or encouraged to look elsewhere for a more 'suitable' placement. Under the SEND code of practice 2015,[3] this is not legal, but it is still happening.

Many staff in settings talk about the challenge of an under resourced system and are afraid that they will not cope, or there will be an accident or oversight resulting in litigation which makes them fearful of admitting a child with more complex needs. This fear can be overcome by developing a strong relationship with the parents and making a joint provision plan. It is also true that sometimes disabled children have their experiences and/or activities restricted for fear that they may hurt themselves or will not be able to fully participate, but it is vitally important that their learning and development is not held back by limited opportunities and practitioner fear. All children need to participate as fully as they can and often solutions can be found by talking plans through with other colleagues, parents and where appropriate the child.

Making sure you are aware of local services and national organisations that can support you is vital so when you work in partnership with parents to make plans, you are informed and committed to the child taking full advantage of all that is on offer.

You should also be able to access advice and support through your Early Years inclusion team at the local authority. The index for inclusion (Booth et al.2011)[4] is a great place to start as it is a tool that will help you identify your own strengths and areas for development, a place from which you can plan and prioritise.

Funding is often raised as a barrier and the situation regarding funding is complex. Childcare providers are expected to meet the children's needs from their existing budgets if they do not have an EHCP, although they can request a top up from the LA if they are struggling to meet those needs. Talk to your area SENCo to find out how this works in your region.

An inclusive image

It is vital that any setting wishing to be inclusive makes it clear and obvious that all children are welcome. It is not sufficient to take a passive approach and say yes to a parent that asks if you can take their child as we know from the research, many will not ask. A full review of your image that you project is needed:

What does your website say about inclusion?

Are there sufficient pictures of children with a diverse range of needs or from a variety of cultures?

Does your SENCo have a prominent place on the website with a welcoming article?

Your vision and values about inclusion need to shine through; this is covered more in Chapter 4 so that any parent of a child with SEND can see that you will welcome them with open arms and work with them to meet their child's needs. By demonstrating your commitment to equal opportunities, you will be making it easier for parents to approach you to talk about their child.

It's natural to have concerns about being an inclusive setting, given the number of factors to consider and the complexities of the system, but there are also a number of real benefits. All children benefit from being in a setting that is inclusive, the childcare setting is their world and in that world it is highly beneficial that they interact with other children that have different backgrounds, challenges and needs to their own. This prepares them for the wider world where they will have already begun to develop an appreciation and acceptance of others as well as developing tolerance and empathy.

Developing practice

■ Develop a strong relationship with the parent/carer – make sure you listen to their concerns and gain their confidence. Ask them to work with you to meet the child's needs.

■ Ensure your outward image promotes the idea that all are welcome.

- Make sure you are aware of the child's interests and preferences and use this information in planning.

- Explore what support is out there to ensure the Key Person and setting SENCo is working closely with the Area SENCo, inclusion team, etc. and able to access any available funding and specialist support.

- Involve parents in the next steps and planning.

- Make sure there is a shadow Key Person who knows and understands fully the child's needs.

- Ensure staff are well trained and if necessary have access to specialist training to develop their skills and confidence.

- Adopt a 'can do' attitude – how can I make this activity more accessible?

- Establish a welcoming environment with posters, pictures and dual language signs.

- Find out about cultural events that are important to the community.

- Make sure your environment reflects and represents different communities, cultures and families – for example, books that show same-sex parents, children with disabilities and different race and colour.

- Ensure transition arrangements are fully robust so the child can move seamlessly onto their next phase or setting.

- Ensure staff are trained in communication and language including Makaton training.

- Audit your practice and provision and make reasonable adjustments to policies and the environment – make it anticipatory and not reactive.

Notes

1 Education Act 1981 (1981) Retrieved 28 July 2020, from http://www.legislation.gov.uk/ukpga/1981/60/enacted

2 HM Government, Parliamentary inquiry into childcare for disabled children, 2014.

3 Department of Education and Department of Health (2015) Special educational needs and disability code of practice: 0–25.

4 Booth, T. and Ainscow, M. (2011) Index for Inclusion: Developing learning and participation in schools. London: Disability Equality in Education.

4 Vision and Values

A TALE OF GOOD INTENTIONS

I once was involved in a project that was supporting children from the Gypsy, Roma, Traveller community (GRT); it was a multiagency project designed to tackle education inequalities in the community. Our vision was strong; we wanted to make sure these children had access to opportunities so that they were not disadvantaged later as the statistics at the time showed that pupils from the white Gypsy/Roma and Irish Traveller ethnic groups had the lowest attainment scores of all the ethnic groups. We were all set about developing a strategy and planning and commissioning support services to realise this vision, but it turned out to be a very rocky road.

Although we all thought we had a shared vision, it became apparent that the values and beliefs of the individual professionals were in fact in conflict. This created friction which inevitably led to a less successful outcome than we had hoped, it didn't completely fail – as some really good things were achieved, but it didn't reach its long-term aim of reducing disadvantage and much of the impact of the work faded away when the funding ran out.

So, what went wrong? In short, insufficient time was spent developing a strong vision, agreeing values and exploring the core beliefs of the team. The housing employees wanted to focus on getting the families into decent housing and the education professionals wanted to work with the families to get them to understand the importance of school so they continued to send their children past the age of 11. These were worthy aims, but other members such as the equality and diversity team were quick to point out that service should not set out to erode their culture and their right to live the lifestyle of their

DOI: 10.4324/9781003016465-5

choosing. They actively promoted the benefit of on-site services, arguing they would be of more value to the community in the longer term and would allow them to preserve their cultural identity and their way of life. Every decision was debated at length and quite often a consensus could not be reached, so progress on the project was slow. Some services even directly undermined other services, for example the local children's centre worked hard to encourage the parents to bring their under 5's to a stay and play session – hoping that this would encourage them to access other services that operated from the building – health visitors, family support workers and midwifery, but a local charity arranged to send playworkers onto the site, so in the end no one came to the centre at all. To me this illustrates that it is not enough just to want the same thing you have to spend time and effort to get under the skin of what it means and develop a shared vision and a clear understanding of your end goal or you will inevitably hit conflict.

To really overcome disadvantage in your setting will require pulling together as a team. You will have to be sure you all want the same thing, share the same beliefs and attitudes and work together towards a common goal. There will be limited success in this if, for example, the leader believes and values all parents as individuals and respects their culture and practices, but other staff do not, and perceive them as being disinterested or uncaring about their children.

This is where your vision, values and mission come into play – spending time together on these three key areas will ensure you all want the same thing, share the same beliefs and attitudes and are prepared to work together to achieve it.

Creating your vision

Getting your vision, values and mission right is crucial to running a successful organisation. It may sound a bit woolly, maybe it does not feel like the real work for an Early Years setting but getting it right is key to success.

The main purpose of a **vision** is to move your organisation forward from where it is now to where you would like to be. It should be aspirational, in that it should aim for an improved state, but also realistic enough that people will believe it is possible to achieve.

In brief terms, it is a statement of how you wish your setting to be in the future.

It is worth spending some time doing this as it is the foundation upon which you build and run your setting. Where do you want to get to?

A vision is like a golden thread that runs through every aspect of your provision, from how you recruit and train staff, to how you set up your environment, plan your provision and work with your parents and community.

Why is a shared vision important?

■ It defines long-term goals and aspirations.

■ It projects an image of success.

■ It contributes to the building of a successful team and expresses the ambitions of a team.

■ It draws people together towards a common goal.

■ It serves as a constant reminder to everyone about what is important.

■ It drives decision making.

■ It is the role of the setting leader to work with the whole community to establish a shared vision.

A vision must be clear and easily understood by all: Key Persons, parents, children, management committee members, governors, visitors, etc. Setting vision statements should direct everyone towards a common purpose and be the guiding force when making decisions. If we do this will it move us nearer to our vision?

A good vision should be:

■ Short – easy to remember

■ Aspirational – not where you are now

■ Exciting – motivates everyone

■ Future based

■ Outward facing

■ Not what you do – but what you will be

Once you have this in place it becomes the driving force of your practice and should be at the forefront of all your decisions. For example, if you decide that your vision is to offer the best early education opportunities for your children you can't do that without recruiting experienced, well-qualified staff and investing in supervision and CPD opportunities. If you decide your vision is to be fully inclusive, then you can't give up at the first challenge that arrives at your door. It follows then that a vision although it is by nature aspirational, it must be something everyone believes in and is willing to work towards. When recruiting staff, you should be able to pose questions that draw out candidates own values and attitudes and assess whether or not they fit with your vision. Whatever your vision is you need to be able to follow it through into all aspects of your provision in order to be able to feel confident that you are moving towards that goal. Once you have your vision statement spend time together establishing how everyone contributes to this; every member of staff has a role. Once when delivering training to a nursery staff I asked them to make a note of how they contributed to the vision and the receptionist said 'I don't have a role in this as I don't work with the children'. The group discussed this and agreed that she was the first point of contact with the parents in the morning, she was the one who set the tone, who encouraged parents who lacked confidence in through the door, who supported the tearful mum who was struggling that day – she had a huge role and hadn't seen it. The next morning do you think she had a bigger smile on her face when she opened the door to let the parents in? What impact do you think that would have? Does the person who cleans your school and setting know that by doing that they are making the environment safe and attractive so children and practitioners can have the best experiences? Everyone needs to know and share the vision and how they fit into it.

Look carefully at the example below:

It is our vision to offer every child the best possible early education experience through inspiring indoor and outdoor activities that ensure they develop a thirst for learning and reach their full potential.

What do you think of it? If it were your vision statement how would you go about making it a reality?

Think about staff, who would you recruit and how would you support them?

Curriculum and resources, what will you do and what do you need?

The environment, is it going to support you in this or does it need work?

Using your vision as a basis for your development plan will keep you on track and guide your decisions.

Values

Have you ever found yourself in a workplace or a situation where you felt really uncomfortable? Maybe you struggled with the way things were run, the decisions that were made and the way people were treated? It is highly likely that this was because your values were not in line with the organisational values. I know for example, I could never work in an organisation that valued profit over people, or one where the leader made all the decisions without consultation; it just wouldn't fit my values and being there would be intolerable for me. If that has ever happened to you, I expect you moved on, or at least planned to if the chance came up.

Your values are deep rooted and personal to you. They provide a lens on how you view the world and a compass for how you treat and respond to those around you. When people judge others badly, it is usually because their values don't match. For example, you may consider the parent who never attends a parent meeting to be lacking interest in their child's education; this is because you as a parent would never do this, your values tell you this is important, but that parent may not see it as important, maybe they are too shy to attend and shows their interest in their child in different ways.

Understanding that your values may be different to others is key to being able to appreciate individuality and being able to treat others with respect. It is highly likely that you will find yourself in a different community or culture to the one in which you grew up and that could cause you to act negatively towards parents or try and influence them to conform to your way of thinking. Listen to the conversations around you and see if you can begin to identify where people are using their own lens and making judgments as a result. Standing back from your own values for a moment will help you to identify why people behave in the way they do and having open and honest discussions about values will ultimately bring to light differences in beliefs and attitudes about pedagogy and practice in your community.

It is important to establish a set of shared **values** that sit alongside and support your vision in the setting. It may include a commitment to overcoming disadvantage, equal opportunities, putting children first, child-centred learning, working with parents, etc. but these are just words and they may take some unpicking so that everyone fully understands what they mean. It is the role of the setting leader to ensure that these shared values translate into practice.

Agreeing a set of values defines the way in which you work and gives a clear message about what you consider important. Spending time as a team discussing and agreeing values is a great team-building exercise and helps to shine a light on potential areas of conflict, and in the end people will choose to work in your setting if they share your values, so making them explicit and public is a crucial component in recruiting the right staff.

Spend time looking at questions:

What do you think is important?

What guides your practice?

What makes you act and behave the way you do?

What was your childhood like?

What do you believe about parents?/children?/pedagogy and practice?

Mission statement

A setting's **mission statement** will provide the framework in which a vision can become a reality. A mission statement is therefore operational. It is a statement of how you will reach your vision. They are of crucial importance in **developing an effective and inclusive educational setting.**

Mission statements set out what a setting's intended outcomes are for its children, their development and overall attainments – academic, social and personal. In practice, it is very easy for a setting to lose its overall direction because it is unsure about what kind of setting it is, and what it is trying to do.

Look carefully at this example:

> Our Nursery School provides an excellent foundation on which every child can build their future education within a caring, secure and stimulating environment where they feel valued and happy. We are an inclusive nursery school where each child is given equal opportunity to discover and develop through high quality play-based learning.

If this was your mission statement, how would you make sure it was happening?

What kind of staff would you employ?

What training and CPD would you provide?

What would the environment look like?

How would you plan the curriculum?

What does high quality look like and how would you ensure you delivered it?

How would you work with families?

How would you work in wider child-centred partnerships?

How are you going to do it?

A mission is about the action you will take to achieve your vision, using your values to guide you.

Staff CPD, parent partnerships, robust recruitment, inclusive practice, community links, multiagency child-centred, partnerships are all key considerations in your mission statement.

CASE STUDY – BUILDING EFFECTIVE TEAMS USING VISION AND VALUES

Little People Nursery had a new manager – Juls, and she quickly noticed there was some conflict in the team. She immediately set up supervision processes and uncovered many sources of this conflict, rotas that were perceived to be unfair, management responsibilities that favoured certain members of staff, CPD opportunities unfairly allocated, arguments about practice and staff resentment towards those that appeared not to be pulling their weight. It was a mess and every time she thought she had solved something it opened a new 'can of worms'. In the end she decided to get help from a professional coach who helped her see that she needed to go right back to the core reason they were there and develop a vision and set of values to help them reach it.

It was a slow process which took many staff discussions over the following term. Getting the staff to agree what they would like to achieve was much harder than Juls thought. In the end they came up with one statement that everyone agreed with

'Every child deserves to have the best we can offer'.

It was a start. They then started to look at how they could make that happen; they considered staff experience and qualifications, what staff did in the sessions, the environment, the curriculum, the needs of individual children, etc. and despite all the conflict they did start to pull together.

In the end they agreed on a vision statement:

'Little People Nursery enables all children to thrive and to develop their capabilities as confident successful learners'.

This was a pivotal moment, as each person was encouraged to consider their role in this and how they needed to work together to make this happen. Juls started to share more of the decision making and staff could see the reasons behind decisions and they began to see why things needed to be done in a certain way as they all linked to the vision to ensure children were able to thrive and develop their capabilities. Decisions around who needed to attend CPD events, changes to the outdoor area, mixing up of staffing rotas, etc. became more straightforward as they all had a core purpose guiding them. Staff seemed to have a new enthusiasm for the work and worked better together as a team. The vision statement was revisited and reconsidered regularly and was used as a starting point for discussions in supervision.

Developing and reviewing practice

Do you have a clear vision for your setting?

How have you identified your values?

Does your mission statement support you to reach your vision?

Could every member of staff tell you what the vision is in your setting?

Following the three steps below will give you your vision, mission and values. The important thing then is to see if everyone agrees, what do parents think? Gather their thoughts and ideas and review them in light of their feedback. Once you are happy with them they need to be used to plan every aspect of your provision to ensure what you do matches what you say, what you believe in and where you want to be in the future. Review these regularly, at least once a year to see if they continue to reflect what you believe and what you stand for.

An example process for establishing vision, mission and values

Step 1 – Create your vision

Explore with staff, governors, committee, etc. This could be in the form of a staff meeting where you discuss in groups the answers to the following questions:

1) What kind of setting do you want to be?
    Write down the keywords and phrases that describe your ideal setting.
    Think big, be bold, be brave!
2) Now break it down –
    Link concepts/reduce duplication
    Pick words carefully
    Can you make it into a paragraph?
3) Now a sentence or a phrase that sums up your thoughts

Note this is a process that is valuable in its own right, don't be in a rush to get to the end, ensure everyone is happy and agrees before moving onto the next step. Keep notes on flipcharts so you can do back and review and check you have captured everything you need to. Work on your vision statement until everyone agrees it captures everything about what you want to be.

Making it short and succinct helps people to remember it; some of the best vision statements are just a few words.

Example vision statements

Oxfam: A just world without poverty (5)

Feeding America: A hunger-free America (4)

Human Rights Campaign: Equality for everyone (3)

National Multiple Sclerosis Society: A World Free of MS (5)

Alzheimer's Association: Our vision is a world without Alzheimer's (7)

Habitat for Humanity: A world where everyone has a decent place to live (10)

Oceana seeks to make our oceans as rich, healthy and abundant as they once were (14)

Make-A-Wish: Our vision is that people everywhere will share the power of a wish (13)

San Diego Zoo: To become a world leader at connecting people to wildlife and conservation (12)

Step 2 – Think about your values

Spend time considering these and making a list of all the things that are important for you – and go through the same process honing down, reducing duplication until you get a list of values you can all agree on. Create a 'we believe in' list to display on your website and in your setting. Again, this is about process, not just getting to the end. Talk about your values – what do they mean in practice? If inclusivity is in there – what does that really mean? If you value parental partnerships how will that look in practice? Do you believe in risk? What does that mean for children in your setting? Many settings produce a graphical image of their values (see Figure 4.1).

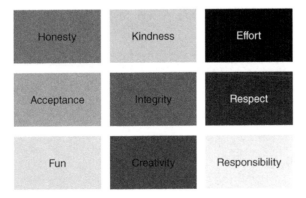

Figure 4.1 Core values

Step 3 – Create your mission statement

Using your vision statement and your values come up with a statement that says how you will achieve your vision, i.e. what you do – your mission statement. Again, this is best if it's short, but if you have trouble getting to something succinct, you can make it longer or use a list of bullet points.

Mission statement examples:

1) 'We create happiness by providing the finest in entertainment for people of all ages, everywhere'. – Disney
2) 'We have absolute clarity about what we do
    "WE SELL HIGH QUALITY FOOD AND BEVERAGE PRODUCTS"'.
    – Pepsi
3) 'We make the world's information universally accessible and useful'.
    – Google
4) 'We are building a place where people can come to find and discover anything they might want to buy online'. – Amazon
5) 'Our core purpose is to create value for customers to earn their lifetime loyalty'. – Tesco

Parent Partnerships

5

MRS SINGH

When I first started teaching there was one big problem that I hadn't antici-pated, and one I certainly hadn't been trained to deal with – parents. I don't remember a single discussion or lecture on the subject in three years of teacher training, so to say I wasn't ready for this aspect of the job was an understatement. I found their demands on my time to be annoying – anything from answering questions, late pickups, rude demands for missing jumpers, having to ask again for dinner money all drove me crazy, but nothing was as bad as the chaotic morning routines. The cloakroom was small and cramped and parents would swamp in with their children to help them with coats, hats, boots, etc. This really annoyed me – how on earth were children going to manage to put their coats on, take them off and hang them up during the day if the parents insisted on doing it for them? My mission was to develop inde-pendence so children were confidently able to manage their personal needs and that was obviously the right thing to do, but I had a hidden agenda – secretly my mission was to get rid of parents as quickly as possible, they got in the way, clogged up the space and even tried to talk to me! In fairness I didn't have a TA, not many people did in those days, and so I had to focus on the children and didn't have time to talk to parents as well. However, I know that even if I did have the time, I have no doubt that I wouldn't have wanted to stop and chat; parents needed to just go away so I could get on with the real job of teaching their children.

My plan was simple – I had a chart on the wall of the cloakroom and a child could get a star if they managed to take off their coat and hang it up and two stars if they came in on their own. I was there to praise loudly

DOI: 10.4324/9781003016465-6

and enthusiastically whilst sticking on the stars and gradually the pressure was on for children to come in alone. Good job! Or so I thought at the time.

Now I know better and I regret the missed opportunities that I let go, the opportunities to get to know parents and build a relationship to bring them in and make them welcome; I may as well have stuck a sign on the door 'parents not welcome'. My intentions were good, but I was sadly ignorant about the importance of parental involvement in their child's education and completely unaware that as a Reception class teacher, I had the power to set the tone for those children's educational journey. What if the real job was not just to teach their children, but to develop a partnership with the parents so that we could work together to ensure their children got off to the best possible start to their education? If this was the job I had definitely failed, and things didn't change until I met Mrs Singh.

A year or two later I was teaching a Reception class with a large number of families with English as an additional language. I enjoyed the challenge but was amazed at how many parents were hanging around in the morning. This was worse than before; these parents were coming into the classroom and sitting down! – I needed to get going and I was not about to 'perform' in front of a group of parents, so time for another plan. I made a big thing of saying loudly to children 'time to say goodbye to mum/ dad grandma etc' and gradually they got the message and they began to leave. Three weeks into the term, they had all gone, all except Mrs Singh. Mrs Singh made no attempts to leave and was completely oblivious to my increasingly unsubtle hints to do so. She came in with her daughter Susan, hung up her coat on Susan's peg and sat down with her. How on earth was I going to get her to leave? Soon she was joining in all the activities and even began getting things ready in the classroom, as she became accustomed to the routines. She was quite useful, so I gave up asking her to leave and we settled into a kind of informal 'classroom assistant' arrangement, but there was one big difference – Mrs Singh joined in everything, reading activities, writing , spelling, etc. – she was learning alongside her daughter and was proud of her own achievements. That seemed to me to be quite a good idea, after all where else was she going to improve her English? But there was another difference emerging, Susan was doing really well, her vocabulary was soaring and she was making rapid progress with her reading, much more than her peers. I still hadn't joined the dots though; I put it down to Mrs Singh who was better able to support her because she was clearly interested in school, lucky Susan.

If only the other parents were as interested and took the time to support their children – then they too would be making rapid progress. It was sometime later when I tried to talk to parents about reading with their children at home, that it hit me. One parent just shook her head and virtually ran away from me, 'I am not teacher'. The truth was Mrs Singh was in school because she was lonely at home, she hadn't stayed in school because she was interested in helping her child, she developed an interest in helping her child because she was in school! She was learning and beginning to understand the way school worked and how her child was learning, so she could see clearly how to support her. The other parents lacked confidence and were afraid to help in case they did something wrong, 'best leave it to the professionals'.

I knew that I needed to get these parents involved and engaged, so they could build their own confidence and, in turn, support their child. This seemed like a great plan until I realised that up until that point, I had harnessed all my energy into getting them to go away...

Parent partnerships are now recognised as being crucial for children's healthy development and their future success and are very much central to the Early Years Foundation Stage (EYFS) in England. It is widely accepted that parents are the first and most enduring educators of their child; of course, this isn't surprising considering that 86% of children's learning takes place outside of the classroom; parents obviously have a huge role to play.

Harris and Goodall[1] conclude that the greatest impact on children and young people's learning arises from the things that parents/carers do with them at home, so it is not hard to understand that if you have someone behind you, encouraging and supporting you in something you will be at an advantage. The culture you are brought up in and the things that are valued in that culture usually has a profound and lasting influence on you. It follows that the more engaged parents are in the education system, the more likely their children are to succeed.

Evidence from Charles Deforges' longitudinal study demonstrates the importance of parents and carers in their child's ability to learn, with up to ten times the influence of teachers[2] in their early years as demonstrated in Figure 5.1.

Developing these partnerships is not an easy task, however, as we know there always seem to be some parents who cannot or will not engage fully with the setting or support their child's learning no matter how hard you try.

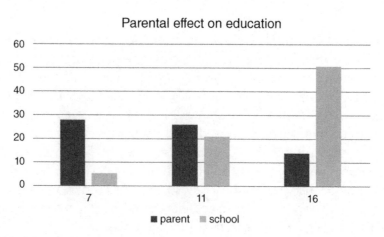

Figure 5.1 Effects of school compared to effects of parents.

So is it just a lottery? – if you happen to have supportive parents who can give you time and encouragement you will do well and if you don't – are you destined to underachieve? Clearly this cannot be acceptable, but the fact remains that many parents are not engaging with their child's education and it is their children that are at risk of poorer academic outcomes. Of course, not everyone can achieve at the same level, but we should believe that everyone with the right influence and support can achieve to the best of their ability.

Most settings have good parent engagement strategies and go to a great deal of time and effort to try to get parents in, offering them many opportunities to attend and interact through both planned and informal events. Although it is great to see that thinking has gone into how to involve parents, there is a fundamental problem in this approach in that it can lead to parents being viewed and treated as a passive participant in the life of the setting. A strategy that asks little more of parents than to turn up is unlikely to be successful in engaging them as learning partners. Parents need to be seen and treated as fundamental to the successful outcomes for children, and their engagement and contribution integrated into all aspects of setting life considered and planned for.

The term engagement is also in itself problematical – what does it mean? Do you measure success by the number or percentage who venture over the threshold or respond to requests? Maybe attendance at parents' evenings means they are engaged? Or the ones who send back the tear off reply slips to letters?

Whatever measure you use for engagement none of them have a guaranteed impact on learning, just because someone shows up doesn't mean that they are truly engaged in supporting their child's learning. The truth is engaging parents is simply not enough, if we really want to harness the power of the triangle of success (setting, child, parent) you need to go much further and start to think of parents as equal partners and encourage and support them in this process. This links directly to the culture of the setting and how it perceives the value of parents. How are they talked about? Are they given opportunities to influence policy and practice and are they listened to? How are they encouraged and supported themselves? When they are invited in, do they immediately think there is a problem? Is there a balance of information sharing or is it all one way? Which activities are popular with parents and which do you struggle to get them to attend?

Considering these questions and others in the same vein will give you an insight as to the culture that exists regarding parents in your own school or setting and maybe some ideas about how to make changes. Planning for parent partnerships needs to be embedded in the whole school improvement strategy and led by the needs and differing contexts of the community. It needs to be intrinsically linked to the attainment and progress of the children – a team approach for all involved.

However, many settings report that although they recognise the value of parental partnerships, they find engaging parents challenging[3] and time consuming.

There are many social and economic factors that conspire against some parents having the will or capacity to engage more fully. Barriers include lack of time, transport, working patterns and of course the 'hard to reach'. The problem is that labelling someone as 'hard to reach' implies that they have a set of shared characteristics – that is, they won't engage, and so it is tempting to try and find a common solution to the problem. In reality, they are not a homogenous group; each parent is an individual with their own unique set of circumstances that prevent them from being involved including different levels of education, health and experience and they come from a variety of contexts which have led to their own individual values and beliefs. Although in practice teachers and practitioners will inevitably adapt the way they approach and engage parents on an individual basis, this can lead to them being perceived as hard to engage or not interested in getting involved if they don't engage in the 'right way'. But not all parents know what is expected of them, often they are unsure of what to do or say, or are lacking in confidence, or simply don't understand their role. For many it could just be that they are rushing around too much to conform to pre-conceived ideas about how they should engage in the setting and they are just relieved their child goes through the door happily.

If we really want parents to engage, then we surely must consider it to be the role of the setting to support the parents as well as supporting their child. Only by taking time and effort to build a strong relationship with a family, based on trust and respect from day one, can you begin to build the pathway to future partnership. If the culture of the school or setting is one of 'we are equal partners in the education of your child and we value you' from the very first encounter with the parents, it helps to set the tone. It is worth looking at your induction processes and considering the balance of information and power here; are parents being encouraged to contribute their ideas, share key information about their child and have their concerns listened to, or are they just given information? How often do you ask your parents if systems like induction are working or how they would like them to be improved?

It is also worth checking signs, website material and letters home, as well as systems and procedures for tone and message. You cannot build a mutually respectful relationship if you send clear messages of superiority making parents feel inadequate.

It is very easy to come across as dictatorial and the use phrases such as 'parents must' or 'must not' only reinforce the perception that you think parents need to be told what to do or even told off.

If a parent who is struggling to get their child to school on time because they are finding it difficult to manage is met with an overly authoritative sign 'latecomers must sign in at the office' they may choose to keep their child at home rather than face having to take them to the office to explain and be 'told off' for being late.

Common issues for example parking, use of mobile phones and lateness are much better addressed by using a respectful tone that explains the problem and then picked up individually where necessary.

Even simple signs such as 'greet your child with a smile not a mobile' can make a parent feel inadequate. It could be a parent uses their mobile to hide their anxiety around being around other people so they don't have to talk to anyone. At the very least a sign like this will annoy and alienate some parents.

If the time is taken to listen to the parents, treat them with respect and be sensitive to their needs and circumstances, it can help to build a relationship upon which barriers can be slowly removed. This requires a proactive approach that is outward facing and reaches out to develop relationships with the whole family, signposting them to other specialist support when necessary and a commitment to strong and effective multiagency working.

But how do you do this in practice? The significant body of evidence[4] pointing to how important it is for parents to be involved in their child's education continues to increase and every teacher and practitioner knows this to be true; yet everywhere I go I ask teachers and practitioners if they have had any training in how to develop learning partnerships with parents and so far, I have never met any who have. So how can staff be expected to just know what to do? Currently we seem to have a culture which assumes parents will engage and when they don't; resource intensive and often expensive strategies are employed to try and 'support them'. These include special workshops and parenting classes – many of which can be perceived as threatening and carry a stigma and often just sound like hard work.

Instead of investing in expensive strategies to target parents – a radical rethink is needed and a more sensible approach would be to ensure all staff were trained in developing learning partnerships with parents, so this can become embedded practice from day one.

Considering how important it is and how it affects the long-term educational outcomes for children isn't it time we supported those involved in education in how to develop partnerships that go beyond just turning up? After all it is a golden opportunity when their child is young, to develop the skills and confidence to support them throughout the whole of their education, helping them to achieve their full potential.

For partnerships of this quality to happen in all schools and settings you need two things: well trained staff who are both confident and competent in developing parent/carer partnerships, and parents and carers who understand their role and are confident and have the capacity to support their child.

The first involves investment in training and professional development, the second is undoubtedly a lot more complex. The Child Poverty Action Group reports that currently 30% of the UK's children are living in poverty[5]; this is a blight on family life and causes inertia. It is not simply that these parents and carers do not know or understand how or do not want to support their children; they simply may not have the energy or at times, the mental capacity to do so. Many families are living in chaotic circumstances due to financial, social or health pressures and for them just getting through the day and feeding their children may be enough of a challenge.

When considering parents who are perceived as not doing enough to support their child, it is easy to jump to quick off the peg solutions. Recommending activities for parents and carers to undertake with their children or investing in resources such as apps that encourage learning songs or rhymes or giving out free books can further undermine a parents' confidence and although these are great ideas, it's a bit like giving someone a new purse when they have no money; it simply doesn't address the route of the problem so will not solve it. There is already a wealth of resources out there to support parents and carers who are motivated to play with and support their child's learning and development, so the problem is not so much about those who don't do it, but about those who can't.

Experience and instinct should tell us that these parents need less of being told what to do and more support to navigate the challenges they face daily. This can only happen where they have the opportunity to develop a close relationship based on mutual trust and respect with someone who can encourage them to get involved, as well as signposting them to what services and support are out there to meet their own needs. This links directly to point one, if all teachers and practitioners were trained in building parent/carer partnerships, there would be a significant reduction in families that are perceived as 'hard to reach' or 'reluctant to engage' and an increase in parent/carer capacity to get more engaged and involved.

Parents/carers, like their children, are unique and each one brings to the school or setting their own individual strengths and needs and their own set of values, beliefs, attitudes, background and circumstances. Being aware of and understanding these factors give clues about how to get them engaged and taking the time to understand their context and cultural norms also provides a great starting point to getting them involved. Partnership approach to working with parents is proven to have an impact on the home learning environment and makes the difference in improving outcomes for all children, particularly those who are vulnerable to disadvantage. Knowing the importance of working in partnership with parents and having training in how to do it well is the key to better outcomes for children.

The two solutions of trained staff and confident parents and carers are actually interdependent and when they come together successfully is when the great ideas and extra resources can be introduced into the family; only then will we be able to move towards a better home learning environment for all children.

This creates quite a challenge, but if you consider that the parental influence on the child's learning is far greater than the setting on its own, it is surely worth the extra effort and maybe the answer is closer than you think. The EYFS framework is now so well-known and embedded in early years practice that most practitioners do not need to refer to it very often and when they do it is usually to remind them of something or confirm some detail. But it is sometimes worth revisiting something you know well with a fresh pair of eyes to consider it from a different angle and ask the question – is there anything else I can learn from this? For example, using the overarching principles in the EYFS as a lens to supporting parents could be useful and may even be a better starting point than the traditional parental engagement policy.

A unique parent

As practitioners we recognise the uniqueness and individuality of children. Parents, like their children, are also unique and each one brings their own individual strengths and needs. Every parent will bring their own set of values, beliefs, attitudes, background, and circumstances to your setting. Being aware of and understanding these factors will give you clues about how to get them engaged and taking the time to understand their context and cultural norms will give you a great starting point to getting them involved. As well as discussions around routines, sleep and mealtimes talk about the wider family context. Use their strengths and interests as starting points for activities and invite them in to share their experiences, anything from baking to yoga will do! Technology can also be a useful tool, ask parents to take pictures of things that interest their child or members of the family and any family events – these can be displayed so that children can talk about their home and their lives outside the setting and parents have something to talk about with you as well. It is important to consider each parent's unique circumstances and talk to them about what they need from you, so take time to ask parents how they would like to be contacted, what information they would like shared and how they would like to be involved. Try to look for the reasons behind parents' reluctance to engage – for example, if you think about parents that just 'drop and run' you might try and solve this by inviting them in for a chat, but a busy working parent will need a very different approach from a parent who is too shy to speak to anyone. They both appear to present the same behaviour, but the underlying context will give you a clue as to their individual needs.

Positive relationships

This is perhaps the most important principle, as without positive relationships the other three principles will have little or any effect on engagement. It is vital that you take time to build respectful, open and honest relationships with parents and try to understand their context and circumstances; this will build trust and once this is established engagement for some parents will be much easier. The role of the Key Person is to ensure that every child's care is tailored to meet their needs and we need to think about our parents in the same way if want them to engage. This means developing good listening skills and being nonjudgmental – you will need to demonstrate that you are there to support and that you are on their side. This is of course easier said than done when you see and hear things that go against your own beliefs and values, but understanding that most parents do want the best for their children is a great starting point. Keep an open mind and be willing to listen and offer support is vital as developing a relationship with parents based on mutual trust and respect is the cornerstone of the partnership between practitioners and parents/carers. Parents have vital and unique knowledge about their child's needs and by building trust with them they will be much more likely to share information with you as well as asking for advice and support allowing you to be able to influence positive change where needed. The health warning with this one is of course the child's safety – if you have concerns at any time over the safety of the child in your care, you must always follow the agreed safeguarding policies and procedures.

Enabling environments

The environment needs to be comfortable and relaxing if we want parents to feel comfortable about coming in and engaging with us. For childminders you have a special 1-1 relationship where the parent comes to your home, you can use this to your advantage, as there will be no need to sit on a tiny chair at a small table, but this is something to consider in a larger non-home base setting. Make regular appointments for parents to come in and meet with you, take the time to explain how things work, including policies and procedures as well as what happens with their child in your setting and how this can be enhanced at home. Share the child's learning journey and discuss how parents might contribute to it through photos, texts or wow cards when they have seen key areas of learning themselves. Do not forget to ask parents about key family events so you can acknowledge them in the setting. These informal meetings can be used to share information about upcoming events such as nursery/school admissions, any referrals or multiagency meetings procedures for early identification, referrals and transitions. Some parents may prefer to meet without their child present or at a time when they can relax and talk without having to rush home to get the tea ready, so offering flexibility is important. Consider also the parents for whom English is an additional language – they may want to bring an interpreter, or it may be a good idea to offer written information in their home language – there are a number of apps that will do this for you.

There will no doubt be times that parents ask for your help and support in accessing wider services, try to keep on top of what is available in your area and have a selection of appropriate information at hand so that you can signpost to specialist services when necessary. The Family Information service and local GP surgery are good starting points for this.

Developing and learning in different ways

We know this to be true about children, but it applies to us all. Different parents will have different levels of understanding and different capacities for learning. Some may know a lot about the Early Years and EYFS framework, others will know very little. Keep things simple, don't overload them with too much information and avoid jargon wherever possible are good principles, as is asking them questions to confirm their understanding when you have shared information of any kind. If the time arises that you must share concerns about the child's learning and development be mindful that different parents may react in different ways to these concerns – some with gratitude, some with denial and others even anger. Carefully consider your knowledge of the parent and be as sensitive and supportive as you can be to ensure messages are heard and reinforce that you are wanting to help. Try not to make any presumptions about how parents might be feeling and certainly do not voice these – the truth is you may think you know, but in reality no one really knows how someone else feels, so give them time to come to terms with what has been said and allow plenty of space for it to sink in and for them to ask questions. The more time and effort you have put into the relationship, the easier it will be.

Technology – can it help?

Most people have access to technology on the go these days and it has the added benefit of being time efficient and non-threatening for those parents who are busy or find engaging face to face difficult.

Many settings tend to 'information bomb' parents with written communications that get lost or forgotten, so having a one stop shop where parents can find the information they need, when they need it can be really useful.

Website

Make full use of your website in terms of making sure that all information that parents need is on there. You can set up secure areas for privacy. This can be easily kept up to date and reduces your need to produce unnecessary paperwork as well as giving you the option to provide information in as many languages as necessary.

Simple things like an events calendar can help parents plan and reduces the stress of having to find old newsletters with dates, etc. Some schools now have online virtual tours of the school and videos around supporting your child with reading, homework, etc. and publish curriculum content, menus, etc.

This way of operating turns your website into a useful source of information and helps to reduce the number of transactional conversations you have with parents, allowing you more time for the important relationship-based type of conversations.

Text

Sending texts to parents to give them snippets of good news can be a very effective way of increasing engagement.

Email

At the time of writing we are in the middle of a coronavirus pandemic and many schools have had to quickly adapt to using online solutions to teaching and learning. It would seem sensible to continue to use these once schools reopen for example use online portfolios for parents, children and school to share homework, upload work and comment on documents or parents can upload photos and videos of children talking about trips/events at home.

Communications planning

Producing a clear plan for how to set up two-way communication with parents is well worth the investment. That way communication is planned for purposeful and valued. Thinking about what needs to be communicated when and how is a good starting point. Considering the type of message is also really important; the more serious the impact on the recipient, the more careful you may need to be, for example, sending a text to convey bad news would not be desirable. Perhaps less obvious and equally important is giving due consideration to the balance of communications, how many good news stories do you send home? How do parents share information and communicate with you?

Taking the time to develop respectful and supportive relationships with parents will enhance the learning and development of the children in your care, not only while they are with you but hopefully long after they have moved on. In truth, these ideas are not new; I have just framed them in a different way and hope that by doing so it will encourage you to think about parental engagement in a different way. The EYFS key principles if we relate them to parents can hopefully give us a new perspective to parental engagement, moving from a blanket policy to a more individual tailored approach. We need to make sure that we recognise the unique circumstances and individual needs and contexts of every parent, that they feel valued and supported as partners and that they know how they can be involved.

It really will be worth the effort.

Developing and reviewing practice

- Develop strong relationships with parents from the start – treat them as partners – make the setting a place they feel comfortable in and engage them as partners from the start.

- Ask parents to tell you about their child and their aspirations; this will give you a hook to develop a partnership.

- Share accurate information about their child's progress and discuss how parents can support the learning at home, be prepared to share ideas and resources.

- Invite parents into the setting for events that are non-threatening, stay and play, story time, etc. – model good practice when they are there and provide ideas for follow up at home.

- Give parents a wide range of ways to be involved – think beyond PTA and parent governors or committee members.

- Ask parents for their communication preferences.

- Give parents various options for communicating and sharing information about their child.

- Make full use of your website and online portals.

- Develop an online communications policy that fully considers data protection and safeguarding.

- Always consider the format of the message – the greater the impact, the more important it is to do it face to face.

- Avoid communications that tell people how to behave or shame parents – always address individual issues individually in a respectful way.

Notes

1 Harris, A., Goodall, J. (2008). *Do Parents Know They Matter?* Engaging all parents in learning, *Educational Research*, 50(3).
2 Desforges, C. with Abouchaar, A. (2003). The Impact of Parental Involvement, Parental Support and Family Education on Pupil Achievement and Adjustment: A Literature Review. DfES Research Report 433. Available at: webarchive. nationalarchives.gov.uk/2013040323 4550/education.gov.uk/publications/eOrderingDownload/RR433.pdf
3 Centre for Longitudinal Studies (2010) *Millennium Cohort Study*. London: Institute of Education. Available at: www.cls.ioe.ac.uk/text.asp?section=000100020001
4 Goodall, J., and Vorhaus, J., with the help of Carpentieri, J. D., Brooks, G., Akerman, R., and Harris, A. (2011). *Review of Best Practice in Parental Engagement Practitioners Summary*.
5 Households below Average Income, Statistics on the number and percentage of people living in low income households for financial years 1994/95 to 2016/17, Tables 4a and 4b. Department for Work and Pensions, 2018.

6 Children with Additional Needs

Brendan was a child who had had a tough start in life. He arrived in my Reception class with his foster mum, who seemed anxious and shy. She knew we were going to be in for a 'rough ride'. Brendan's behaviour was unpredictable, ranging from attention seeking to, on occasions, behaviour that was a danger to himself and others. The plan was to use the behaviour management policy and reward Brendan as much as we could in school but follow through with sanctions for unwanted behaviour. It seemed a good plan, after all that's what a behaviour policy is for – to train children to learn to behave in acceptable ways. Well that is certainly what I thought, and I set about setting up sticker charts and publicly praising Brendan as much as I could. The next few weeks were exhausting and the system was time consuming, but that would have been fine if it had worked, it didn't and not only that, it began to have a negative effect on the rest of the class. Children started to ask for stickers and point out how good they had been; one parent even asked me why her daughter, who was good all the time, had fewer stickers than Brendan. Brendan's foster mum hid away from the other mums as their children regaled tales of Brendan climbing on and jumping off tables, knocking down displays and kicking members of staff, and he wasn't on any birthday party list. Clearly, I needed to rethink my approach, but how was I supposed to do this when all I had was a policy that was failing him?

My breakthrough happened the day he pulled some pictures off the wall, and I launched into my usual script of how sad that had made me and how sad his friends were, and I ended by asking him 'now do you have anything you would like to say to me?' This is a well-used phrase by teachers to which

DOI: 10.4324/9781003016465-7

children almost always reply 'sorry!' and they look a bit sad. It is like a code that children learn from early on and it allows both parties to draw a line under the incident. Knowing what I know now, it was ridiculous to expect Brendan to know 'the code', he had developed strategies to ensure he got the attention he needed by behaving in a way that caused an adult to react. No one had ever really expected him to be sorry, they had just shouted at him and his need for attention was quickly met in that moment. So when I asked him if there was anything he wanted to say to me he looked up and said 'yes, I think I want to tell you about my gerbil', that was the moment I began to understand that this little boy wanted and needed someone to connect with him, listen to him, understand him and appreciate him, not with stickers, but with undivided time and a relationship that would help him feel secure.

After that I spent 20 minutes with him every day at lunchtime talking and sharing toys – and gradually over time things started to improve, although his established patterns were still sometimes in evidence. I will always be grateful to Brendan for showing me that a relationship-based approach is so much more effective than any behaviour management policy and I always took this approach from then on with all children.

We are on a curve of change in the way in which special educational needs are identified and supported in England, following the implementation of reforms to the special educational needs and disabilities (SEND) reforms in 2015.[1] For Early Years settings, these changes have mostly led to new and improved ways of working, but they also presented some new challenges and caused some existing ones to be reexamined under the lens of these reforms.

Before the reforms Early Years settings worked on a system of Early Years Action and Early Years Action Plus and many settings had an expectation that 'Action' in Early Years Action and Early Years Action Plus meant extra staff or one to one support. This is a very costly approach and meant that in some cases a significant amount of time and effort went into gathering evidence that the child's needs were severe enough to warrant them being categorised in the 'Action Plus' category which attracted funding. Not only was this costly, it was time consuming and it led to frustration as many settings felt that they were being asked to stretch their already limited resources to prove their case. The deficit nature of this model meant that when their applications were unsuccessful settings began to question if they had the capacity to meet the needs of children with SEND, leading to a culture of reluctance to accept the child in the setting. This is backed up in the report from Contact a Family[2] that states that 25% of parents surveyed stated that their child was refused a place because of their disability or special educational need and 28% did not think provision is inclusive and supports their child to participate in activities along-side their peers. If children were to be viewed as individuals we needed a shift away from proving how severe a child's needs were to one where every child has their needs identified and met whatever they may be. Once this approach is taken it is easy to see that extra staffing and one to one support is not the only solution.

Under the new reforms settings are encouraged to look more closely at their own provision and practice and consider the individual needs of chil-dren before referring to outside agencies, but this throws up a new challenge as staff may only have fairly low level qualifications and there is no require-ment currently in the non-maintained sector for the SENCo to have an SEND qualification. Typically, Initial training is provided by the Area SENCo team (LA service) and usual practice is that SENCos rely on Key Persons to identify any initial issues and then the SENCo works with them to gather observations. Advice is then sought from the Area SENCo team who work with SENCo to identify appropriate support, give advice and monitor prog-ress of children. Additional support is given by specialist support services as required.

Time is an issue as there is no funding to release staff allocated to the role. Early Years SENCo's report that the processes are very time consuming and are difficult to fit alongside their daily routine and workload. These processes include dealing with confidential paperwork and meeting statutory, non-negotiable deadlines, undertaking observations and supporting Key Persons with their observations, conducting parent consultations and meetings, attending Common Assessment Framework (CAF) meetings and liaising with specialist support services. SENCo's report that the role demands extremely high organisation skills and strong communication skills and the role has a significant leadership element needed to ensure all staff understand the plans for children and implement them effectively. The lack of in-depth training can cause anxiety to SENCo's and lead to some confusion around early identification of need, leadership of effective practice and parental engagement.

Barriers to identification

The new Code of Practice states that identifying children with special educational needs is the responsibility of everybody in a setting. This approach can make identification easier, as a child's Key Person may be better placed to recognise any issues they may have, with the appropriate training. However, there are still a number of potential barriers to effective identification of children with special educational needs in the early years. One very real barrier that they still face is the reluctance to talk about issues with parents; this is hugely challenging if you have never been trained in how to do it and the fear of upsetting parents is real. This upset can have the effect of a parent removing their child to attend elsewhere and of course that is bad for business. Having a strong relationship with the parent where you are already having an ongoing mutual dialogue with the parent is the best way to overcome this issue; this is outlined more in the parent partnership chapter. The other barrier can be a reluctance to label a child; this is best overcome by practitioners being really secure in their knowledge of child development so they are able to identify any development concerns that appear to fall outside the typical parameters for the age of the child. In early years, it is sometimes difficult to distinguish between normal developmental stages, developmental delay and a special educational need. Ensuring each child is given the support they need so they make progress is key and constantly monitoring and discussing with SENCos and line managers so that no child slips through the net.

Being a SENCo

The Early Years Foundation Stage (EYFS) framework has as one of its overarching principles 'children develop and learn at different rates and at different rates', this underpins the fact that the framework is for all children and it is up to the practitioner to ensure the learning needs of the child are met no matter what the barriers may be. The effect of a child having unmet needs will lead to further disadvantage as they go through school, so it is important to recognise them early on and provide the right kind of support to ensure those needs are met.

Under the SEND Code of Practice (2015) each setting must have a named SENCo to ensure that the setting is meeting the needs of all children. If this is you it means that you are considered to be skilled and experienced enough to undertake such an important role in your setting – hopefully you feel proud of that! But the SENCo role is undoubtedly complex; it has a significant leadership element which demands extremely high organisational skills, a good knowledge of child development and SEND and strong communication skills and you would be quite unusual if you weren't a little apprehensive if you are new to the role.

In schools all new SENCos must hold or be working towards a Master's level qualification; it recognises the depth of knowledge and experience required to undertake the role. However, in an Early Years setting this is not the case and you may be a named SENCo but have had limited training and/or experience. That is often in addition to the everyday demands of being a practitioner in the setting with limited or no release time.

How can you make it a manageable role?

There is a wealth of information that describes the role and responsibilities of the SENCo online, but sometimes it's hard to know where to start.

As a new Early Years SENCo there are three statutory documents that you need to have a clear understanding of: The 2015 SEND Code of Practice (COP) which outlines the duties that every setting has in meeting the needs of children with SEND; The Equality Act 2010[3] which sets out the expectations on a setting so that no child is discriminated against or disadvantaged; and EYFS framework, which sets the standards for all early years providers and promotes equality of opportunity and anti-discriminatory practice. These documents are the key to ensuring all children are supported and have their needs met in your setting.

The key principles you need to keep in mind are:

■ To ensure SEN is picked up at the earliest opportunity

■ To support staff to have the knowledge, understanding and skills to identify early and intervene appropriately

■ To ensure parents know what services are available and what to expect from any service they engage with

■ To have high aspirations for all children

■ To support the LA in identifying children with SEND

■ There is a greater focus on all agencies working together to support children and families

■ To ensure high quality provision and high expectations for all children

Getting support

As SENCo, you can feel isolated and even overwhelmed at times, as the 'to do' list seems never-ending and the responsibility of decision making can weigh heavy. To overcome this, try to build a network of people you can meet with, chat to or call when you need support. Start with your own manager and make sure that you are both clear from the start that this role will require you to work together – where you identify issues or challenges you will need their support to address them. Make sure you have time to discuss individual children, areas of practice that you identify need development or training and build in opportunities to discuss your own work/life balance. This is a role that can be all consuming and you will need lots of management support. Next, build a strong relationship with the Area SENCo and any other SENCos you meet on your training, most likely they will be glad of support as well and be keen to say in touch. Consider setting up a regular time to talk and use that time to share ideas and practice. Thinking about where your children transition to can be helpful, make an appointment to visit the local school SENCo and talk about the role and discuss how you can work together. These simple steps will mean there will always be someone to talk to when you are unsure of anything.

The role of the Key Person

The current emphasis is on SEND as everyone's responsibility, not just the SENCos. Arguably this is a positive shift as Key Persons work with children on a day-to-day basis and are best positioned to raise any developmental concerns that they may have about the children in their care. The expectation is that this process is firmly rooted in the settings overall monitoring of the learning and development of all children by the Key Persons. It is worth assessing the strength of the Key Person system in place in the setting to make sure it's as robust as it can be in developing parent partnerships, assessment of children's progress and child-led practice. Often practitioners lack the confidence to know when the right time is to refer for help or may believe a child has additional needs when in fact, they may just need the provision to be adapted to enable them to learn. No assumptions should be made that children making slower progress have SEND and regular conversations with practitioners will help them grow in confidence. Practitioners may also be concerned about labelling a child too soon, recognising that this can be a less than helpful approach, for example, when does delay in speech due to a lack of rich language experiences become a special need? Some special educational needs are also hard to identify early, as normal developmental parameters must be considered. These conversations may raise issues that can only be addressed by working in partnership with the manager to identify areas for training and development across the setting.

The key questions that you need to ask as SENCo are:

- Does the child have a learning difficulty, that is, a significantly greater difficulty in learning than their peers?

- Does the child have a disability that prevents or hinders them from making use of the facilities in the setting?

- Does the learning difficulty or disability call for special educational provision, that is, provision that is additional to or different from the provision normally made available?

Keeping these questions at the forefront will help you to explore the issues with the Key Person and also give them the confidence to be part of the wider discussions around how to meet the child's needs.

Parent partnerships

Parent partnerships are also key, get to know parents well and take the time to build a trusting relationship with them. They may be anxious or unwilling to engage in dialogue with you and this may prove to be the most challenging part of your role, but the most important to get right. It is not enough to just report to parents on progress; now the expectation is that parents will become fully involved in planning for their child's needs so take the time to listen to them, they know their child and if they feel valued they will work with you to support them. Practitioners need to consider the child holistically and in a wider range of contexts than just the setting and this is only possible if you are able to speak confidently with parents.

Some practitioners lack the confidence to have 'tricky' conversations with parents; they are worried about upsetting them, labelling children too early, or even that they will remove the child, so they steer away from anything that may cause concern. Now, however, not only are they expected to be having those conversations, but they are expected to work as partners with the parents, requiring them to utilise a set of skills that they may have had little or no training in.

Talk to your manager and start a dialogue about this – how do we interact with parents here? Do we treat them as partners and involve them in identifying next steps in learning? Do we shy away from difficult conversations? What training do we need as a staff to support us in this area? (see the chapter on parents for more ideas)

Voice of the child

Another key partner that is often overlooked is the child; their wishes, views and feelings are central to the COP, but that is often overlooked with very young children or those who have communication challenges. Key Persons should be using their observations and interactions to discover children's interests, their likes and dislikes and discuss these with parents to get a complete picture of the child, this can then be taken into consideration when planning for their next steps. Using this information as a starting point for discussions with parents can be really helpful as they focus on the child's strengths and abilities first; this makes the meeting much less threatening for parents who are then much more likely to engage in the process.

Getting organised

SENCos often report that the processes are very time consuming and are difficult to fit alongside their daily routine and workload. These processes include dealing with confidential paperwork and meeting statutory, non-negotiable deadlines, undertaking observations and supporting Key Persons with their observations, conducting parent consultations and meetings, attending CAF meetings and liaising with specialist support services.

So, you are going to need to be very well organised – use your network to look at how they are managing the role and develop systems and processes that work for you in your setting. This will support you in setting up a filing system that is simple and useful. Start with the things you must do, then the things that are considered best practice so it is more manageable. Make sure you familiarise yourself with local and national organisations that can support you and the families you are working with. Consider mapping out the year so you can see when key events are happening and discuss any pinch points with your manager, allowing plenty of time for deadlines and organising meetings. Work with your manager to ensure that each Key Person's supervision is focused on the needs of the children and that evidence of need and progress are recorded through this, so you are not scrambling around for information at the last minute. Talk to your colleagues and manager regularly so there is ongoing dialogue about children and how and where to adapt provision to meet their need as well as sharing the decisions about when to refer or ask for help.

Children attending your setting may have a wide selection of needs, ranging from severe and complex to quite minor. The more complex the needs of the child, the more specialist support and advice there should be, and so following that and working in partnership is key. However, it is quite likely that you will have children that do not meet the threshold for referral and quite often these are the children who can slip through the net, without having their needs met. It is vital that these are picked up early on if we are to close the disadvantage gap.

It is worth a special mention for childminders here as the choice of a child-minder is often an attractive proposition for a parent of a child with additional needs. The take up of the two-year-old offer of funded early childhood educa-tion and care (ECEC) for the most vulnerable and disadvantaged children including those with SEND could be the modern equivalent of the community support network, especially if it is offered by childminders, who have the poten-tial to build up a close and supportive relationship with parents and carers. A childminder can play a really valuable role in supporting families that have to navigate their way through support services as they can be an advocate for the child and family in what can be a quite daunting process.

The most common areas of need in young children in early years settings that are not always fully met are:

■ Behavioural, social and emotional difficulties

■ Speech, language and communication difficulties

Some children will have needs in one of these areas, but many will have needs in both as they are intrinsically linked – that is, if you can't communicate verbally or process information, then you are more likely to use behaviour to communi-cate how you feel.

Understanding behaviour

We all know that a child's behaviour can be challenging, our own children can frustrate us and try our patience at times, so how do you cope when you're car-ing for someone else's child and they are driving you mad? Children have to learn to behave, just as they have to learn to read, write and count, and adults must work together to facilitate this learning. Very few children need specialist intervention for their behaviour and understanding the child and the family, promoting the behaviour you want to see and responding to their needs in a nurturing environment is usually all that is needed.

Challenging behaviour is just a physical way of expressing a need. It is often due to a heightened emotional state that has caused a child to feel anxious scared or frustrated and they have not yet developed the resilience to cope with their feelings or the vocabulary to express them clearly. Sometimes it is due to a learned pattern, for example, its only when I scream or kick does my mummy take notice of me; that was how Brendan used behaviour. Understanding the reasons behind the behaviour is the first step to supporting children to self-regulate. Self-regulation is the ability to manage your own emotions and behaviour in an appropriate manner in the context of the situation. It is not hard to think of examples where adults have not been able to do this, so to expect it of a young child is unrealistic. Self-regulation skills need to be taught and should be central to any Early Years practice; this can be done by providing calming spaces, planning in activities and ensuring adults fully understand how to co-regulate with children that need it. Supporting a child to develop appropriate and acceptable behaviours is not a quick win; it will take time and patience.

The good news is that there are three steps that if followed through can make a real difference when it comes to supporting children to manage their behaviour in a positive way – Promotion, Prevention and Intervention – each step is designed to be built on, that is, you do not stop promoting when you move to prevention, and both these continue if you move to intervention.

Promotion

Most children will respond well to promotion. This means making sure children see and hear the behaviour you would like them to adopt. It's easy to make the mistake of focusing on the negative behaviour and reprimanding children, in the hope they will stop 'doing it', but you don't learn how to do something by being told what not to do, you only learn by practicing the skills you need to learn. In Early Years behaviour is intrinsically linked to child development, so look carefully at the age and stage of the child to make sure your expectations are in line and that you plan in activities that will support them to move on as they grow and develop. A nurturing environment will create a climate for positive relationships to grow and success relies on focusing on positive interactions supporting engagement; giving clear instructions within simple to follow routines and providing ongoing and consistent encouragement to learn.

The most important thing about promotion is to ensure you have taken the time to develop a shared ethos with the parents so that you work together to develop a partnership approach. By understanding their approach and underlying ethos, you will be able to support them in how to respond to the child's needs, and guide them in establishing responsive and nurturing interactions that will promote the child's social and emotional development. The importance of getting to know the child and family, understanding their routines, culture and context cannot be overestimated in helping you to achieve a consistent approach.

Prevention

Sometimes, however, more needs to be done with individual (or groups of) children and they may need to be supported through prevention strategies. They may well need extra support in self-regulation, expressing and understanding emotions, problem-solving and developing social relationships, requiring an individualised approach. Your daily plans may need to include activities that focus on development in these areas. Keep in mind that all behaviour is communication and when a child is 'behaving badly' they are simply expressing a need they haven't yet learned to communicate in a more appropriate way. This may be in line with their development, so it is worth considering their stage of development, not simply their age, and what their next steps are. Labelling the child 'naughty' doesn't help – it does nothing to explore why it happened or to look at the idea or feeling that the child wants to communicate, so observing carefully and noting the things that happened just before the unwanted behaviour can be a useful strategy and help you reflect on why it happened. If a child is angry or upset, they cannot engage in a reasoned conversation, so it's best to use co regulation techniques and wait for calm and ask them what made them feel the way they did, this can help to build the vocabulary needed to start to express emotions.

Keep a record of incidents and analyse it carefully for patterns. Record what the behaviour was, where and when it happened and what else was happening at the time, to see if you can identify any 'triggers' and note context. It can be helpful to log incidents using four key terms – **appearance** – what it looks like, **rate** – how often it happens, **severity** – how severe is it (bear in mind age and stage – a two-year-old biting maybe low level, but a five-year-old may be more severe) and **duration** – how long it lasts. These strategies will help you put plans in place to prevent incidents occurring and give you an idea of what activities you can plan to support growth and development.

Intervention

A very small number of children may need to be supported through intervention and need some specialist support. This may be just about behaviour, or due to other special needs or disabilities that require a much more structured approach. If you have explored all the options in promotion and prevention, you may feel it is time to call in specialist support – your Area SENCo is a good place to start to get advice. The work that you have done with the parents should mean that you can have an open conversation about your concerns and that in fact they will not come as a surprise if you have been working together on promotion and prevention for a while anyway. A behaviour support plan will usually be put in place and you will need to work in partnership with the parents – both in terms of contributing ideas and in following agreed plans.

The behaviour support plan includes prevention strategies to address the specific triggers of challenging behaviour; replacement skills that are alternatives to the challenging behaviour; and strategies that ensure challenging behaviour is not reinforced or maintained. The behaviour support plan is designed to be holistic and followed at home, in their care setting and the wider community and to be centred round the individual child's needs.

Speech language and communication

Communication and language (C&L) is one of the three prime areas of learning and development. A prime area is a foundation for learning, and it is easy to understand that children who struggle in this area will be disadvantaged in their learning, unable to fully understand, communicate and read or write to the necessary standard will inevitably result in educational failure and impact their life chances.

Fifty-nine per cent of language-delayed three-year-olds have behaviour problems, compared to only 14% of non-language-delayed children (Richman et al., 1975; Silva et al., 1987).[4]

Two-thirds of young offenders have speech, language and communication difficulties, but in only 5% of cases were they identified before the offending began (Bryan et al, 2009) 20.[5]

Language development begins from birth as they tune into those around them and learn to respond to adults speaking to them and interacting with them – this is known as 'serve and return'. A child's language development at 24 months is an indicator of how prepared they will be to access education opportunities at school.[6] But there is no doubt that some children do not get the kind of stimulation that ensures they develop well in this area and many arrive in their setting with limited skills in speech language and communication.

Assessing children's needs in this area is tricky, developmental norms are wide and it can be hard to work out if a child needs extra support or if they just need more time. Common sense tells us that making sure all adults are well trained in how to develop children's speech and language and offering the right kind of environment and activities to promote development in this area will be of benefit to all children.

The progress check at two is a good time to reflect on whether or not a child is developing typically in this area. Discussing progress with parents and health visitors and how you can work together to look at what the child's needs are and how to meet them is good practice. It may be that specialist support is required if the delay is linked to another condition, for example, autism, hearing loss, getting advice from your SENCo and your Area SENCo will help.

It is also worth remembering that delays in speech and language link closely to emotional and behavioural development and that for many children they go hand in hand.

Reviewing and developing practice

Role of the adult

The adult is the most valuable resource you have; ensuring they are modelling good language and communicating clearly with children, listening to them and responding appropriately and investing time in them is key to language development. Ensuring every adult is well trained is important, but there are many simple practices that, when done well support children to develop well. Ensuring parents understand their role in this is also important, the chapter on parents will give you ideas on how to engage with parents to develop a partnership approach, making conversations around development for example limiting the use of dummies, much easier.

Invest time

Spend time chatting to children about what they are doing, make it natural not a running commentary or a series of questions. Introduce new vocabulary though natural interactions and extend through play experiences e.g. if they say they are building a tower you could say 'that's a really tall tower' – or 'ooh I am going to build a tower next to your tower'

Give children time to respond and process instructions. It is the serve and return of conversation that develops children's processing skills and builds their vocabulary.

Research has also shown that serve and return builds brain architecture, when a baby makes a babble or a gesture –' a serve' and the adults respond with attention or words – 'a return', neural connections are built in the brain. This is central to development of speech, language and communication skills. This is so important that where interactions are negative or just absent it can have a serious effect on brain development and lead to the impairment of physical and mental health.

Songs and rhymes

The rhythm and rhyme in songs helps children understand the structure of language and promotes early literacy skills.

Books

The more the better, children who are ready to build up an early understanding of language patterns and are constantly being introduced to new and interesting words.

Sustained shared thinking

This is when the adult and child work together to solve a problem or clarify their thinking, supporting deep level learning, evaluation and critical thinking. The adult gets to model their thought processes so children can develop these skills. Phrases such as 'I wonder what would happen if…' or 'why don't we try…' are examples of sustained shared thinking, but it's important to remember that the child is leading not the adult, so keeping to their agenda is key. Be careful not to ask too many questions as it can interrupt the flow of conversation.

Modelling language

Speaking clearly, slowly and facing children when you speak is crucial. If a child says a word incorrectly or uses the wrong word, rather than correct them, just repeat it back in a correct way, for example, a child may say 'I want to pay aside' you can say 'oh you want to play outside – ok let's go.'

Use of other methods of communication

Not all communication is verbal; long before a child learns to speak, they will be able to communicate through the sounds they make, the looks on their faces or their gestures. Even after speech is developed our bodies, gestures and looks continue to express meaning and even when the speech says one thing and the body language expresses something different it is the body language that we know to be the truth. It makes sense to make use of these visual cues when developing communication skills in children as they support the development of spoken language, listening skills, comprehension and receptive language skills. Makaton is a system which combines speech, signs and symbols and is widely used to support the development of communication skills in children, particularly benefitting those that find verbal communication frustrating or challenging. Using a system such as Makaton alongside other visual cues such as visual timetables to demonstrate routines will enhance the communication skills of all children in the setting.

Role play

Almost all settings have role play areas set up, but quite often they are underused as a learning resource. Ensure they link to the child's experience and spend time playing with them to develop their understanding and build their vocabulary.

Reviewing and developing practice:

- Review your Key Person system, do you spend enough time with parents and getting to know the needs of each child?

- Work with parents to create a plan for their child and set regular review times.

- Ensure all staff know and understand about brain development and how to support children to learn to self-regulate.

- Make speech, language and communication a priority in your setting – ensure all staff are trained in sustained shared thinking.

- As a SENCo, make use of local networks for support.

- Use an audit tool to help you prioritise your areas for development – ECERS[7,8] or ITERS may be useful.

- Plan as many real-life experiences as possible and talk about them.

Notes

1   Department for Education (2015) *Special Educational Needs and Disability Code of Practice: 0 to 25 Years.* Department for Education.
2   Contact a Family, *Levelling the Playing Field: Equal Access to Childcare for Disabled Children,* November 2015.

3 The Equality Act (2010) Available at http://www.opsi.gov.uk/acts/acts2010/ukpga-20100015-en-1.Google Scholar

4 Richman, N., Stevenson, J. E., and Graham, P.J. (1975). Prevalence of behavior problems in 3-year-old children: An epidemiological study in a London borough. *Journal of Child Psychology and Psychiatry, 16*, 277–287. [PubMed] [Google Scholar]; Silva, P. A., Williams, S., and McGee, R. (1987). A longitudinal study of children with developmental language delay at age three: Later intelligence, reading and behaviour problems. *Developmental Medicine and Child Neurology, 29*, 630–640. doi:10.1111/j.1469-8749.1987.tb08505.x

5 Bryan, K., Freer, J., and Furlong, C. (2007), Language and communication difficulties in juvenile offenders. *International Journal of Language and Communication Disorders, 42*(5), 505–520.

6 Roulstone, S., Law, J., Rush, R., Clegg, J., and Peters, T. (2011). Investigating the role of language in children's early education outcomes.

7 Andersson, M. (1999). The Early Childhood Environment Rating Scale (ECERS) as a tool in evaluating and improving quality in preschools. Studies in Educational Sciences, 19.

8 Clifford, R. M., Russell, S., Fleming, J., Peisner, E. S., Harms, T., & Cryer, D. (1989). Infant/Toddler Environment Rating Scale: Reliability and validity study-Final Report. Chapel Hill, NC: Frank Porter Graham Child Development Center, University of North Carolina at Chapel Hill.

7 Ready to Read?

A LOVE OF READING

As a teenager my first proper job was in a library and my main responsibility was to put the returned books back on the shelves in the right place. The books were heavy, and the library was huge, so I was always grateful when I was asked to go and shelve the books in the children's section. Two reasons, the books were lighter, and the room was smaller, but really, I loved it most because the books were just wonderful. The covers were enticing, the pages were beautifully laid out and they constantly surprised and engaged me, and I confess to many times when I just stopped working and sat and read. It was here that I began to be fascinated by children's books and that fascination has never left me; I watched the parents come in with their children and babies and snuggle up to read to them before taking their chosen books home and I remember the sights smells and the warmth of a truly enabling environment. I got to know the families and watched the children come back week in week out for more, I knew they were enjoying books and knew that this would help them learn to read. It wasn't just the quality of the books though, it was the experience and the emotional connection that developed through this simple act of sitting together and snuggling up with a book – it was bound to make the child feel safe and connected and therefore associate reading books with love and find it a deeply satisfying experience. I did not think at that time, as it was beyond my experience and imagination, about the children who did not attend the library or who never had a story read to them, I do think about them now – quite a lot.

I remember very clearly teaching children to read back in 1980 when I started my career. In those days we were very reliant on reading schemes that

DOI: 10.4324/9781003016465-8

gradually built vocabulary, giving confidence to children to develop their skills over time. The reading scheme dominated the classroom and the teaching and left little opportunity to look at or enjoy other books. In fact, it might be hard to believe, but there were only two 'real books' in my classroom when I started. – *The tiger who came to tea* and *Rosie's walk*, both wonderful books but it hardly constituted a library. The children did learn to read and went on to achieve good academic results, but did it inspire them to want to read? Probably not. Every day I would call over a child to read to me, usually pulling them away from a more exciting and interesting task, and we would sit down to find out what Jennifer Yellow Hat had been doing or what had happened to Roger Red Hat and Billy Blue Hat – (yes, really that was what they were called!) in The Village with Three Corners. It was efficient enough as a method, but was never going to excite the imagination of the average five-year-old, so it came to no surprise to me when one day a small boy complained 'Do I have to?? Reading is boring!' No surprise, but a bit of a wakeup call nevertheless, – How could reading be boring? That's like saying travel is boring, surely it depends on where you go and what you do whether or not it's boring. Well, I clearly wasn't taking them anywhere exciting – and it was then and there that I made up my mind to bombard them with beautiful, interesting, exciting books that made them want to pick them up and read. Trips to jumble sales, libraries and car boot sales followed and soon everything we did came from and led to stories and books – we built a curriculum around their interests, enthusiasm and excitement. No child in my class was ever going to say reading was boring again!

And guess what? – they thrived, the results were fantastic – children wanted to learn to read so much they would romp through the reading scheme books! I will never forget the day a child came to me with 'The very Hungry Caterpillar' and proudly announced he could read it and he did – every word. Once a child asked me 'what will happen when I've read all the books there are?' – I was thrilled by this question – what did I say? 'trust me you won't run out!'

Ready for school?

Children in the UK are amongst the lowest age in the world when they start school. This was a decision first made in 1876 on the Factory Act's recommendation, to stop child labour, resulting in making school compulsory for children aged between five and ten in 1880. In fact, only 22% of the world's children start school so early and almost all come from former or current commonwealth countries, as the British influence spread. Since that date we have steadily increased the school leaving age, so that more children have a wider range of opportunities to support them into work. This begs the question why has no one looked at the other end, the starting point? Why are our children starting so young, with what is after all, the legacy of Victorian decision making based on an emerging need for safeguarding?

Some would argue that the earlier they start, the better; it gives parents more opportunity to work and there may have been some merit in the economic argument in the past, but now that many working parents in England are entitled to 30 hours funded childcare from three years of age, this is somewhat outdated. There is no evidence to support that starting school earlier improves educational outcomes, if it were true the UK would have one of the highest performing education systems in the world. According to the PISA[1] results published by the Organisation for Economic Co-operation and Development (OECD) in 2016 we are currently ranked in the 15th place for Science, 26th place for Maths and 23rd place for Reading. Of course, there are many other factors at play as to why our children are doing as well as they could be, but it is clear to see that them being there earlier is not giving them any advantage.

Why does this matter? It matters because we now have a clear understanding of how children develop and learn that we perhaps were not so clear about in the Victorian age, and that the systems, culture, pedagogy and practice that are commonplace in schools do not always support the developmental needs of children nor do they enable their learning. You could argue that the building is not the important factor, but what happens inside and the culture ethos and vision that the school holds around early education, and indeed there are examples of good practice.

However, this is not always the norm and it is not uncommon to see reception aged children in school sitting for long periods of time on the carpet or at tables doing their 'work' and made to complete tasks for which they are not developmentally ready, inhibiting their development and preventing them from learning. The Early Years Foundation Stage (EYFS) is built on the characteristics of effective learning, playing and exploring, active learning and creating and thinking critically. If you think about it this is how we all learn isn't it? Think learning to drive, or baking a cake or learning to sail, you learn by doing not by sitting and watching, or by cutting out and labelling pictures.

The increasing pressure schools feel under to improve their results is resulting in a top down approach whereby children are required to sit still, hold pencils and complete a range of, often inappropriate, adult initiated tasks in order that they are better prepared for Key Stage One. Indeed, the new Reception baseline Assessment (RBA) has conceded that learning in Reception classes needs to be more in line with Key Stage One, because a significant number of children are still not meeting the early learning goals, which are deemed to be the bench-mark for school readiness and the National Curriculum. No one appears to be asking the question why this is the case, nor are they considering the possibility that it is the Key Stage One curriculum that needs to be brought in line with the EYFS, so that more children can develop at their own pace and succeed.

Of course, many schools do value play-based learning but they are increasingly torn by the real challenge and pressure to improve results, so they make every effort to get children ready for the demands in Key Stage One in the hope that this will improve results. This is a flawed approach, as we know that to learn, children need to have their needs met and that means ensuring their physical and developmental needs are met too. The Reception Year is still part of the EYFS framework and many children who are disadvantaged by background, challenge or need still need to be focusing on the prime areas of learning as outlined in the EYFS. Unless they are secure in these areas they will have problems accessing the more formal learning associated with Key Stage One.

The love of reading

Becoming a lifetime reader is dependent on developing a love of reading[2] and few would argue against the fact that the ability and motivation to read impacts on the life chances of all children. That emotional connection that I witnessed in the library that helps children to develop a love of books can be fostered through careful consideration of practice, ensuring all children get to experience the joy and wonder of books to hook them in and keep them reading forever. Without it my fear is that reading could be seen as a chore and some children will quickly disengage. Evidence tells us that children make the best progress when they are taught through a structured phonics-based system, but does this really do the job of creating inspired lifelong readers? My experience tells me that, for some children, it is not enough, and we somehow need to be able to create that rich emotionally rewarding connection with books for all our children if we are to make them into readers.

Parents are regularly described as their children's 'first and most enduring educator' and reading is the one area of education where it is just assumed that parents will pitch in and support, both in terms of reading to their child and hearing them read. But the reality is many do not do this and it's not difficult to see that a child who has been read to from birth has a great advantage over one that has had very limited experiences in this respect. As educators we are somehow expected to get children to read at a broadly similar age despite the obvious impact of wildly different starting points – so how can this be achieved?

Despite significant emphasis and quality teaching, some children are not making the progress they should be and there are stark inequalities in the attainment findings[3] with a 15% gap in the Phonics attainment for children on free school meals compared with their better off peers.[4] There are those who argue that there will always be some children that do better than others, as we are not all born with the same levels of intelligence, but this isn't an intelligence gap, it would be ludicrous to argue that those from poorer households are less intelligent, but nevertheless they are not doing as well as other children and poverty should never be used as an excuse for failure.

Every teacher recognises the children that come into school ready to read. They can speak fluently, listen attentively and engage and respond. They sit still, do well at phonics and build up a good sight vocabulary of tricky words, generally they make good, steady progress. They usually have smart book bags that come back and forwards every day and reading records that are filled in by parents that show an interest; these children become good readers almost naturally.

Then there are those that are not ready, the ones who have a limited vocabulary, find it hard to listen and concentrate, don't pick up phonics or keywords quickly and often forget their book bag or it's clear no one has read with them at home. Is it the fault of the parents? This is certainly the view of some teachers who sigh at the lack of the book bag coming into school, or the one that is transported to and from school without it ever being opened in the home.

The evidence is clear that the parental role is hugely important in developing children's attitudes to and skills in reading:

"Early reading experiences with their parents prepare children for the benefits of formal literacy instruction. Indeed, parental involvement in their child's reading has been found to be the most important determinant of language and emergent literacy (Bus, van Ijzendoorn & Pellegrini, 1995)."[5]

Those children that are finding reading easy are usually the ones that have been talked to and read to since their earliest days and this has laid the foundations. They know about books, they understand the structure of sentences, the flow of a story and appreciate the wonder that books hold. They love the special bond that develops between adult and child when books are shared and understand that they are a great joy. In short, they have been exposed to a rich reading environment – they are ready to read.

Not all children are so lucky; some children come from homes where reading is a very low priority and some where there are no books at all. These children are not ready, the foundations have not been laid and they are at a huge disadvantage from the start. Teaching these children phonics is a bit like teaching someone to decode a foreign language before they have really appreciated what it sounds like and why you need to learn it. We then put them through a system in school, whereby their success seems to rely heavily on the support they get at home, which further compounds their disadvantage. Some parents have poor literacy skills and struggled themselves at school and we expect them to support their child's reading, fill in the reading record and become an active partner in the whole process. One easy way to deflect the anxiety that this causes is to opt out of the process, after all reading is much better left to the experts isn't it?

One of the key aspects to teaching is working out what children can do already and what they need to do next. Reading is no different, if a child has little or no understanding of books and reading for pleasure then this is where we need to start. We need, somehow, to be able to compensate for all they have missed out on and give them the foundations they need, the same foundations that the 'natural' readers have had, quite a challenge, but if we do not acknowledge the different starting points of children then we are certainly doing them a disservice.

Using a systematic synthetic phonics approach is heavily promoted by the UK Government and features in Ofsted's Bold beginnings report

> all primary schools should make sure that the teaching of reading, including systematic synthetic phonics, is the core purpose of the Reception Year.[6]

This system ensures children are taught the skills they need and then given the books at the right level to practice their skills, develop their confidence and learn to read. This sounds sensible and is very effective practice for some, but not for all. Some children struggle to pick up the phonic code and for them reading is often a frustrating process. These children are often fed a diet of uninspiring texts that are simplistic in their structure and lack the wonder and inspiration of beautiful, well written books. They quickly work out that 'reading books' are levelled and they are on a lower level than their peers. This leads to a lack of confidence as generally speaking, your skills in reading are highly visible at home and in school and sometimes to other parents as well. Teachers are then encouraged to target the children who are not doing so well with extra phonics and more practice texts, which causes frustration and boredom with the whole process.

What if that is all you get? What if you never really get to be exposed to the wonders of books? Suppose reading is just a chore to you and you just don't get the point? We all need to understand the point, the bigger picture, what we are trying to achieve. When we learn to drive we don't just learn because we have a desire to operate pedals and gear levers, we think about the places we will go and the freedom and convenience being a driver will bring us. No chef ever got inspired to learn to cook by being exposed to a daily diet of dry biscuits, and endless tests about which knife to use when; it's the sights, smells and flavours of the banquet that makes them say 'I want to do that.'

It is the same with reading, children need to know the joy and pleasure it will bring and why it is important to learn. They need to understand that they can find out about things that interest them through books and that, particularly in these days where there is an over reliance on screens, books can be a delightful experience that feeds all the senses. Once you appreciate the end goal, learning the skills becomes much less arduous. Teaching synthetic phonics works and has been responsible for an overall rise in standards, but it needs to be set in the context of the bigger picture where children see the point and have a desire to learn to read. Just as a chef needs the skills to cook, but also the vision of the reason why they are having to work so hard to learn – the lure of the banquet.

But what do you do for those children who have not had the foundations laid out for them? How can you compensate for lost time? Expecting parents to suddenly start doing something they have never seen as a priority before seems to be a bit optimistic, why would they suddenly start reading with their child?

So much emphasis is placed on the teaching of skills that fostering the love of reading and books has tended to become a much lower priority. Traditionally, story time was and still is a part of the curriculum, but how much time and effort really goes into choosing the book, and planning to make it a rich and exciting experience? How many classrooms have beautiful reading corners, stocked with a wide variety of books that reflect the children's interests? Often book corners appear neglected and have tatty old books in them, that do nothing to inspire the children, nor do they teach them that books are a precious and valuable resource.

Nowadays it is very common to see a structured organised approach to phonics firmly embedded in the timetable in Reception and even nursery classes and this has meant that reading results have improved overall. No one is suggesting that we stop doing this, but for those children who are disadvantaged on entry and then further disadvantaged by the systems we employ to teach reading this isn't enough on its own. Once reading becomes seen only as a 'subject' we miss opportunities to enrich the experience and engage children in the process and to weave it through their daily experiences. Those children who need more sensory learning experiences or more physical play could be taught reading in the woods by jumping across logs with letters on re-enacting 'We're Going On A Bear Hunt' or by using shaving foam to form letters and say the sounds. These very simple examples are beginning to diminish from some classrooms, as the scheme they are using is deemed to be doing the job and the reading lesson is over and done with by 9.30 every morning.

Why would you practice dance steps until your feet ached if you never got to dance for pleasure or watch a ballet? Why would you practice scales on an instrument and play the same tune repeatedly if you hadn't experienced the sound of an orchestra? Why would you work so hard in a kitchen just to be able to name all the equipment and bake biscuits repeatedly for no particular reason until they were perfect? Unless we place reading inspiring books at the core of our practice some children will continue to struggle to see the point.

Reading has a profound impact on children's academic success. Those that can read well are better able to access the curriculum, make more progress and achieve better outcomes. But that is only part of the picture, children that learn to love reading develop their creative skills and their imagination through books and they are able to access wonderful places and escape to magical lands – quite simply reading should be a joy. Take the time to just spread the joy and read as much and as often as you can to your children, so that they get hooked for life – it could be the most important gift you give them.

Reviewing and developing practice in reading

- Are your books beautiful and well cared for? – this sends the message they are valuable. Do you promote how special they are and teach children to care for them and they are stored in a way that is easy for them to manage?

- Do you include books that reflect children's interests and experiences?

- Books can be part of any area in a setting or classroom including outdoors – they don't solely belong in a book corner – does your environment promote reading everywhere?

- Do you include and reread old favourites?

- How do you introduce new books? Books need to be introduced with enthusiasm and time spent discussing them before they go on display.

- Do you know what your children's favourite books and stories are?

- How often do you share books with small groups, pairs and 1-1. Some children might need this every day.

- Let children be comfortable – don't insist they sit legs crossed – it's not a time for training.

- Use story sacks and other props to encourage further play and connection.

- Invite parents/carers/grandparents etc into story sessions and let them just enjoy sitting and listening to them with their child.

- Let children and parents choose books to take home and share.

- Encourage children to bring in books.

- If you are near a library arrange visits and get parents to come along.

- Make books with the children that they can share at home these can be a way of recording visits and events but they create powerful connections for children if they are 'in' the book.

- Make sure parents are hearing the message that reading is fun and value them joining in instead of pressuring them into workshops.

- Never miss an opportunity to model reading stories – some settings even have a reading tent at fayres and events!

- Read, connect and enjoy books as often as you can.

Notes

1 http://www.telegraph.co.uk/education/leaguetables/10488555/OECD-education-report-subject-results-in-full.html
2 Sanacore, J. (2002). Struggling literacy learners benefit from lifetime literacy efforts. *Reading Psychology, 23*, 67–86.
3 Save the Children (2015) Ready to Read, Closing the gap in early language skills so that every child can read well.
4 DfE, 2017 Phonics screening check and key stage 1 assessments.
5 Bus, A., van IJzendoorn, M., and Pellegrini, A. (1995). Joint book reading makes for success in learning to read: A meta-analysis on intergenerational transmission of literacy. *Review of Educational Research, 65*(1), 1–21. doi:10.3102/00346543065001001
6 Ofsted – Bold beginnings (2019).

8 Transitions

TROUBLESOME TRANSITIONS

My first leadership role was head of Early Years in a five-form entry Infant School. That meant that each year we had approximately 150 new children staring in the Reception Classes in September. On taking up my post I noticed that other members of staff called the Reception wing 'The Zoo'. I was shocked at how disrespectful that was, but I quickly realised why the name had evolved. This was long before the days of funded early education and very few children had been to any kind of preschool provision. Settling children and parents in and establishing routines was done in a very ad hoc fashion and little time and attention was given to making sure these children got off to a smooth start. Children arrived at school poorly prepared; basic things like lunches, PE kits, coats, unnamed jumpers and lost book bags seemed to cause endless problems and take up disproportionate amounts of teacher time. Parents seemed anxious and unsure of what was expected of them, children cried, letters in book bags remained unread and reading at home was for most sporadic. This was all compounded by the sheer numbers of children, and the unsettled ones seemed to have a ripple effect across all the others. That said, most problems were ironed out by Christmas, but it still amounted to nearly one whole term of chaos, except for jumpers; they continued to cause chaos, especially in warmer weather.

There had to be a better way! I set about to develop new transition arrangements for the following year; I listed everything that I thought parents needed to know and invited all new parents to a meeting during the summer term. Around the room I had tables set up, one with lunchbox ideas, one with a PE kit, one with a book bag and reading books, etc. I also had someone on hand to

DOI: 10.4324/9781003016465-9

help them fill in forms and make sure they took away a full suite of important information documents. It was a busy marketplace event that finished with a talk from me with slides. I clearly remember this being the first time I had ever produced a presentation – not on a computer, but an overhead projector. The evening went well, almost everyone had attended and I gave a thorough talk about school routines and expectations. I felt really proud that I had solved a major problem; parents now had all the information they needed, and I looked forward to a smooth start in September. It was a well thought out and executed plan, except it didn't work; I hadn't solved anything at all. In September parents still seemed clueless, PE kits didn't arrive, school meals were unpaid, jumpers were still unnamed, and children still cried. Looking back, I can remember feeling very irritated, I had given them all the information they needed, what on earth was wrong with these parents? The answer of course is there was nothing wrong with them; I had just not considered their needs or the needs of their children well enough. I had been so focused on what the school needed from the parents, I hadn't even thought about what the parents, or even the children, needed from the school. I hadn't built in any kind of relationship-focused activities or given parents a chance to speak; it was totally a one-way process.

Realising my error, I began to think about transition into school in a completely different way. I began reading and researching best practice and trying out new things, trying to get it right for every child and family so their start in school was a positive experience. I focused on each family and put systems in place that meant they got to know the teacher and the teacher learnt about them. One thing I learnt very quickly was that good transition was much less about telling people what they should do and much more about listening to what they need

What is transition?

Transition is defined by the Webster dictionary as 'a passage from one state, stage, subject or place to another' and is usually viewed as an event that happens for children at the end of the summer term. But transition involves change and that throws up a common problem – change is challenging and needs to be planned for carefully. Most people would agree that change can be a difficult process if it's not prepared for and handled well. Adults often struggle with change, even when it's something they have planned for, look forward to and can see the benefits of. For example, imagine you have been working in a job you like, with people you get on with and you are clear about systems, processes and expectations. Now think about getting a new job, maybe you went to visit and had a look round, but by the time you got there to start you had forgotten a lot of what was explained to you. Everyone seems very nice, but you do not know them, and they don't know you and they do things very differently. There are different expectations, equipment, rules and lots of new people to meet and learn about and you are keen to make a good impression, but actually you are left feeling a bit overwhelmed and on occasions inadequate. It is not unreasonable to expect that your productivity would probably dip in the first few weeks, while you adjust to your new role.

Now imagine how this feels for a small child, dependent almost entirely on the adults around them to feel safe and secure and not yet having the skills or resilience to cope with major changes in their life without support. Making successful transitions in the Early Years is key to achieving successful outcomes, developing processes and activities with individual needs in mind and building confidence and resilience is key to this. If children do not feel safe and secure, they can't learn as they may be in a constant state of anxiety. It may take weeks for them to settle and not only does that mean their learning is limited, it is also setting them up for more anxiety later when they make further transitions.

Transition is not just a physical move to a new setting or a new room; it needs to be about aligning practice, developing shared understanding and building bridges for children to cross, not hurdles for them to leap over. It is not an event but more a way of working that ensures children do not have to face large amounts of change all at once.

How to implement transition successfully?

Transitions actually happen more often than you may think, moving from one activity to another, getting ready for lunch or going home are all examples of transitions. Taking the time to plan through introducing change gradually will be important steps to success. The more confident and reassured a child is the quicker and easier they will settle into their new environment or activity and the faster they will be able to fully access the learning opportunities. It is also worth noting that the more vulnerable and disadvantaged a child is the more difficulty they will have adapting to new situations and new relationships and surroundings, which can act as a barrier to engagement and learning. Until a child feels emotionally secure, they will be in a state of either fight, flight or freeze and while this is happening their 'learning brain' is in shutdown.

Most schools and settings have transition policies, but the downside of this is they often follow a prescribed process and treat all children the same. They usually comprise of a timetable of events that children, staff and parents attend, but not all children and families are the same, some will need more support, for example, extra visits, and some may need something completely different. Successful transitions need to be bespoke to the needs of children and families so that each child is able to smoothly move onto the next stage in their learning with their needs being met. For this to happen it is essential that you spend time knowing and understanding each family context and fully understand the needs of the child. Some children may need more visits, or to be accompanied by a parent; others may need to have individual systems and plans put in place before they arrive. As well as knowing the child and the family knowing and understanding the previous and next setting is needed. The EYFS is one continuous key stage and the more practice can be aligned throughout, the better it will be for the child's learning and development. Of course this throws up challenges; it will not be easy to liaise with multiple settings or schools, but some very simple changes to systems and processes can help to shine a light on the children and families that need more support, and getting it right for them is crucial to good outcomes for the child.

Working with staff from other settings, discussing children, sharing policy and practice all help to align practice, so that change is built on what has gone before and what comes next. This can be easily overlooked as so much transition planning focuses on planned events, but in reality needs to be an ongoing established system, for example, a termly network meeting. One of the key recommendations in the Hundred Review (2017)[1] concerned transition and promoted this view:

> In order to establish an effective transition into YR, it was strongly believed that this was best viewed as a process that emphasised continuity rather than a single event.

The four key principles from the EYFS are a useful lens to help you plan your transitions:

- A unique child – keep in mind every child is different and some will need more support than others to make successful transitions. How will you find out about children's individual needs in time to put transition plans in place for them?

- Positive relationships – all adults working together makes for smoother transitions – parents and carers and professionals understanding the impact transition will have on the child with a key focus needs on involving parents as an active partner in the process.

What systems will you need to change to ensure parents are actively involved in transition and their voice is heard?

■ Enabling environments – taking the time and trouble to align practice so that the environments are similar in terms of provision and expectations. Are you fully aware of what the environment is like where your children are coming from or going to? What steps do you need to take to work towards alignment?

■ Children learn in different ways and at different rates – consider the child's holistic needs around all aspects of care and learning. How do your systems help you know and understand the child really well?

These four key principles may be part of the EYFS framework but are equally applicable to all ages and provide a good starting point for thinking on this subject.

Connecting with parents

Many schools lament the fact that some parents do not fully engage in their child's education; there are many reasons for this, and they are outlined in more detail in the chapter on Parents. But it is worth considering in this chapter that parents don't know what to expect and usually behave according to the norms set down by the school. If you want parents to engage then, allowing them and expecting them to engage from their very first contact with you makes sense, it sets the tone. Holding events such as the one I described at the start of the chapter does little to engage them; it sends out a clear message we are in charge and we will tell you what you need to know. As I found out, information events are not enough to really engage parents in the process and in the wider learning community. Taking the time to build a trustful and respectful relationship, asking parents to tell you about their child so you can get a picture of them, their likes and dislikes, favourite toys and their personality will help you prepare activities and an environment that they will instantly feel at home in, with activities that engage and enthuse them. As you get to know the family you will be able to pick up on any anxieties and provide tips and strategies and signpost for any extra support needed so that measures to support are put in place. If you can do home visits for this it is ideal as parents are on their 'home ground' and more likely to relax and talk.

There will be a need for a lot of information but consider how and when this information is needed (see the chapter on parent partnerships for more ideas).

Most parents do not want to be inundated with too much information at the same time as it can be overwhelming. Information about the setting can be prepared and updated regularly if kept online and shared with parents in this way.

You will soon get to know parents that don't have access to technology and those who may need information in a simpler form or a different language, so these can be prepared in advance as well. The key is to make sure parents know where and how to access information as and when they need it.

The case study below demonstrates how the key person tuned into the needs of the child and the parent and put in place a plan to support them both. This individual approach was key to ensuring the child settled in happily. The relationship between the parent and the Key Person was sufficiently developed that they were able to have open and frank conversations with the parent so that she could see her role in helping her child settle successfully at nursery.

CASE STUDY - JOSH

Little Tots day nursery has a relationship-centred approach to transitions with the Key Person working alongside the parents and carers to develop an approach that's right for the child. Josh was a new child starting at nursery in September and Debs was assigned as his Key Person, so she visited Josh and his mum Sue at home prior to him starting. Josh seemed happy and played contentedly with his toys, while Sue and Debs talked. Sue spoke enthusiastically about Josh, about his interest in cars and things with wheels and about how she was going to miss him when he started nursery, it was clear they had a strong bond. This was hardly surprising since Sue was a single mum and there was only the two of them in the home. Debs took the time to listen to Sue who explained that she was worried Josh wouldn't settle and that he would make a fuss when she left him. Debs began to realise that Sue was anxious about leaving Josh and knew that if she didn't support this transition well, both Josh and Sue could have difficulties.

Debs arranged for Sue and Josh to visit together and stay as long as they needed and gradually distance herself from him in the setting. She made sure there were toys and books that reflected his interests so that he would engage quickly. Debs also supported Sue to understand that voicing her anxieties could affect Josh as he was bound to feel anxious about her leaving if she was unsure about it herself. Debs helped Sue develop a positive routine and vocabulary around starting nursery using phrases like 'today is nursery day – you will have a wonderful time', 'we are nearly at nursery and you will have a great time' and 'I am going now, but I will be back to collect you when you have had lots of fun with your friends'. Deb also explained to Sue the importance of avoiding any negative talk about nursery when Josh was around. She was able to do this well because she had built a trustful and respectful relationship with Sue and responded directly to her concerns. Sue was happy to leave Josh and he settled into nursery really well with no problems.

Connect with children

Getting to know children well is key to good transitions and the Key Person system is designed to make sure that relationships are secure between children, the family and the setting. If you can undertake a home visit and really take the time to listen to their parents talk about them you will build up a picture before they arrive for any settling in visits. Good early years practice starts with what you know about the child and how you can use their interests and natural curiosity to enhance their learning and development; use the information you have gained to plan activities that will spark their curiosity and hook them in. Visiting children in their previous setting and talking to their Key Person can also help to build a picture. Make sure that Key Person staff are allocated well in advance of transition visits so that time can be spent developing a relationship with the child.

Connecting with wider professionals

Taking the time to liaise with other settings and schools where your children will move onto will help you to align practice. Close observation of routines and discussions around expectations will help you to make simple changes that smooth the path for children. Talk to other providers and try and replicate the environment, structure and routines as much as you can so that children get a sense of familiarity where they can. Obviously, you will all need to consider developing expectations and extending learning opportunities, but these sit much better in the context of keeping a sense of familiarity where it is possible to do so. Some schools and settings have SENCo get togethers to discuss individual children, share ideas and create a community of practice. This helps to ensure any individual arrangements for children with additional needs are planned for well in advance and if needed plans for early intervention are made.

When a child leaves you to move onto a new setting, there is usually a transfer document that details the needs and the stage of development of the child. Try and make this document as useful as you can, ensure parents get a chance to express their views and opinions and try and capture the child's voice by including information about their interests and activities they enjoyed with you. Keep in mind the core purpose of the document is to tell you about the child – does your transfer document do this? You may want to consider looking at doing some shared moderation activities with the new setting to ensure assessments are accurate and robust.

There is no doubt that there is a lot of information to be shared at the point of transitions, but it is worth taking a step back and reviewing it using the following key questions:

1) What information do I need to have or to share?
2) What is the purpose of it and does my system do the job?
3) What is the best way to share it? – online, paper copy, secure transfer, website, video, etc.
4) Is everyone's voice captured? – child, previous setting, parent, Key Person, SENCO, external agency.
5) When is the best time to share it?
6) Is it accessible to all? – complexity of language, different languages, use of pictures, etc.?

The following case study shows how, when transitions are carefully planned for, children can make a seamless move from one setting to another. Partnership working, and clear communication can make all the difference to how well children are supported.

CASE STUDY – COMMUNITY OF PRACTICE – MAISIE

Maisie's Key Person noticed she was not making as much progress in her learning and development as the other children, particularly around speech, language and communication. Maisie's communication and language skills were assessed as being typical for a child 22–36 months, even though she was 45 months old, so well below age-related expectations. The Key Person and the SENCo did some joint observations and began to put support in place to improve Maisie's speech and language in the setting and supported her parents with ideas to do at home. The SENCo raised Maisie's needs at the community of practice meeting in May. The school SENCo worked with the setting SENCo to make a referral for some speech therapy as Maisie was due to start school in September. She also ensured that Maisie's new teacher was aware that she would need some extra support, helping her plan to meet her needs. By the time Maisie started school, plans were in place to support her development and she was accessing speech therapy.

Reviewing and developing practice

Use the information in this chapter to review your transition processes – consider:

- The four key principles of the EYFS – how can you use these as a lens to view transitions?

- Do your systems help you know and prepare to meet the individual needs of children and families?

- Do you plan for transitions as a process – not just a one off event?

- Is your practice aligned with settings that come before and after?

- Do you regularly liaise with those settings and discuss children's needs and plans?

- Are parents fully engaged?

- Is your information sharing system giving people the right information, in the right way at the right time?

- What are your plans for reviewing any changes you make, how will you gather the views of all involved?

Books to support children with transition

Topsy and Tim start school – Jean Adamson, Ladybird
Don't want to go – Shirley Hughes, Penguin
First day at bug school – Sam Lloyd, Bloomsbury
Harry and the dinosaurs go to school – Ian Whybrow, Puffin
I am too absolutely small for school – Lauren child, Hatchett

Note

1 Early Excellence, 2017 – Teaching four- and five-year olds: The Hundred Review of the Reception Year in England.

Conclusion

During my career I have worked with many children who were disadvantaged due to their background, the challenges they faced or their needs. Many initiatives have come and gone: the introduction of the 15 hour funded offer, the 30 hour offer, birth to three, the Foundation Stage, the Early Years Foundation Stage, the Sure Start programme, Early Years Pupil Premium, the SEND code of practice and the two-year old offers to name a few.

Despite all this change in practice and the different initiatives and funding streams little has changed. Relative poverty among children rose from 13% in 1979 to 29% by 1992. After a drop in the late 1990s it now stands at 30% – that is 4.1 million children who are living in poverty after the costs of housing.[1] It doesn't seem to matter what amount of money is thrown at trying to fix the problem as little appears to be being done to address the core issues of disadvantage.

This book is not political and of course it goes without saying that poverty is a deeply rooted issue in this country that needs to be addressed but being poor is not in itself the problem; many children from low income homes thrive as they are loved and supported well by nurturing adults. But for some parents, it is the lack of support and the isolation that they feel as well as the overwhelming number of problems and challenges that they have to face alone that prevents them from fully nurturing their child. If you are struggling to get through the day, worried about how you are going to heat your home, feed your child, keep the car on the road so you can get to work and afford to buy the things you need, there may be little left to give in supporting your child beyond meeting their most basic of needs. If you have a child with additional needs and are struggling to get the things they need and providing round the clock care, navigating your way through health services you may not be able to focus on much else.

DOI: 10.4324/9781003016465-10

We have lost our sense of being connected, which is one of the basic human needs. Adults are often disconnected from communities and families and the amount of support available has dwindled away; for many their main source of connection is through social media, which often portrays an enhanced view of the lives of others making you feel even worse. In our brains, we are hard wired to form attachments with our caregivers when young, but sometimes those connections fail causing attachment issues which impact on our ability to form and sustain relationships as we grow into adulthood and hence become unable to form secure attachments with our children, and so the cycle goes on. However, the good news is that it is never too late and that attachments can be made, and our brains can learn to connect better with others.

This is where practitioners come in – the one thing I have learnt from all my different experiences is that you can make a huge impact on a child's life and their future by connecting with their parents. Taking the time to develop strong respectful relationships that are based on mutual trust rather than professional hierarchies enables parents to connect with you and gives them a lifeline of support. You may be the one constant person in that family's life, which is why the Key Person system is deemed important enough to be statutory in the Early Years Foundation Stage. Once those relationships are strong, parents will trust you enough to open up about the issues they face and more willing to accept the advice and support that you may feel you want to offer. The impact this will have on the child will grow and develop, parents will slowly build their confidence and become more involved, engaged and their capacity to support their child will increase. This is where the magic happens; connected families who can get the support they need will be able to significantly increase their capacity to help overcome at least some of the disadvantages that their children may face. Initiatives and funding come and go, but you are a constant and can make such a difference to children's lives. By focusing on the individual strengths and needs of each child and their family, and finding solutions to the barriers they face, you will set each child on an educational journey of success. This book has hopefully given you some things to think about and ideas to try – never underestimate the influence you can have by making small changes. You have the power to change children's lives – you are amazing!

Note

1 Fullfact.org/economy/poverty-uk-guide-facts-and-figures

Index

abuse 6
active learning 25
additional needs i, 27, 28, 62, 65, 89, 93
adult initiate 3, 75
amygdala 7
attachment 8, 18
attainment gap 2

babies 8
barriers to identification 60
behaviour 23, 51, 57, 58, 65, 66, 67, 68, 72
Booth 30
Bourdieu 14, 18

child development 17, 22, 25, 60, 61, 66
child initiated 23
communications 54
contact a family 2, 59
COVID-19 3, 4
creating and thinking critically 25
cultural capital 6, 14, 15, 17
culture i, 8, 14, 15, 16, 21, 25, 29, 33, 34, 37,
   45, 47, 48, 59, 67, 75

disability 6, 59, 63
disadvantage i, 2, 3, 4, 5, 6, 7, 8, 10, 14, 16, 17,
   30, 33, 34, 50, 60, 65, 78, 93

early education i, 10, 20, 21, 35, 36, 72, 75, 83
early learning goals 76
Early Years i, ii, 1, 3, 7, 8, 9, 10, 12, 14, 15, 16,
   18, 19, 20, 21, 22, 23, 24, 25, 26, 29, 30, 34,
   45, 52, 58, 59, 60, 61, 66, 75, 81, 83, 93, 94
Early Years foundation stage (EYFS) 1, 9, 12,
   13, 20, 21, 22, 25, 26, 29, 45, 50, 52, 54, 60,
   61, 75, 76, 86, 87, 91, 93, 94; framework 12,
   20, 29, 52, 61, 76, 87

EHCP 31
enabling environments 52, 87
Early Years Pupil Premium (EYPP) 10, 11, 12,
   13, 17

free school meals 7, 77

'Golden Time' 23

inclusion 3, 27, 28, 29, 30, 31, 32

key person 9, 10, 17, 18, 32, 51, 62, 88
key stage 1, 3, 22, 81

Maslow 8, 9, 18
Mathematics 24
mission statement 38, 42

national curriculum 1
neglect 6

Ofsted 12, 14, 21, 26, 78, 81

parent partnerships i 3, 38, 47, 62, 87
parents 1, 3, 7, 9, 11, 13, 14, 16, 17, 20, 21, 27,
   29, 30, 31, 32, 34, 35, 36, 37, 38, 40, 43, 44,
   45, 46, 47, 48, 49, 50, 51, 52, 53, 54, 55, 59,
   60, 61, 63, 64, 65, 67, 68, 69, 71, 73, 75, 77,
   78, 79, 81, 83, 84, 85, 86, 87, 88, 89, 91,
   93, 94
pedagogy 21, 22, 23, 25, 26, 37, 38, 75
play 7, 9, 19, 20, 21, 22, 23, 26, 34, 38, 45, 49,
   55, 65, 69, 70, 71, 75, 76, 79, 80, 81
playing and exploring 25
positive relationships 51, 86
poverty 2, 3, 6, 7, 17, 41, 77, 93, 94
Pupil Premium 7, 10, 18, 93

reading i, 24, 44, 53, 72, 73, 74, 76, 77, 78, 79, 80, 81, 83, 84
Reception baseline Assessment 75

school readiness 21, 76
SENCo 31, 32, 59, 60, 61, 62, 63, 68, 69, 71, 89
SEND 2, 29, 31, 58, 59, 60, 61, 62, 65, 93
Social Mobility Commission 11
speaking 24, 28, 68, 78
special educational needs 2, 58, 60, 63

talk for learning 24
teacher-led classroom 24

teaching and learning 21, 25, 29, 54
technology 51, 53
transitions i, 22, 52, 85, 86, 88, 89, 90, 91
trauma 6

unique child 22, 29, 86

values i, 3, 8, 28, 31, 33, 34, 36, 37, 38, 39, 40, 41, 42, 47, 50, 51
vision i, 20, 31, 33, 34, 35, 36, 37, 38, 39, 40, 41, 42, 75, 79
voice of the child 64

website 53
wider professionals 2, 89

Printed in Great Britain
by Amazon

28527851R00057